C000045681

Foot Loose
in South Wiltshire

a diary of farming and nature

1936 – 1950

by

Jane Holmes

with a foreword by

Patrick Holden

First published in the United Kingdom in 2007 by
The Hobnob Press, PO Box 1838, East Knoyle, Salisbury SP3 6FA.

British Library Cataloguing in Publication Data
A catalogue record for this book is available from the British Library.

ISBN 978-0-946418-71-8

Typeset in 12/15 pt Joanna
Typesetting and origination by John Chandler
Printed in Great Britain by Salisbury Printing Company Ltd, Salisbury

Foreword
by Patrick Holden
Director of the Soil Association

If ever the time was right for the publication of Jane Holmes's diaries, that time is now. Jane's observant entries take us back to a gentler place of environmental richness and abundance that we hope is not lost forever. Aptly titled Foot Loose, the diaries provide a wonderful glimpse of an age past when a young girl could go off alone bird-nesting, engage with passers-by, or hitch a ride on a lorry without fear.

The prognosis for the Earth and our future is not good. To our great sorrow and shame, the environmental catastrophes unfolding before our eyes are the result of Man's actions.

The area around Wiltshire where Jane grew up and learnt farming has suffered greatly as a result of the post-war intensification of farming – the daily events and descriptions of wildlife and plants in Foot Loose are testament to that. A drastically reduced bird-count, diminished plant species, a fall in the water table – these are the direct consequences of the adoption of farming systems that have sought to dominate rather than work with nature.

Foot Loose is a poignant and heartfelt reminder of what once was, a countryside teeming with beautiful birds and animals in a natural and healthy habitat. Where many country-folk, particularly those whose work brought them into contact with the soil, had an innocence and gentleness of spirit about them that has been lost to our detriment in the intervening years. It is an important and valuable document to remind us of what we have lost through our mistreatment of the Earth and our failure to understand the interconnectedness of all life forms. It is hoped that these diaries will help the Green movement by raising public awareness of what we have lost and, if we take immediate action, still have the chance to restore.

I dedicate this book to Kim who shared with me a deep heartfelt love for the whole realm of Nature.

My thanks

To my daughters Rowena and Georgina for their unstinting support and encouragement and to Georgina for her help with much of the original typing from the scribbled entries long before computers had entered the household.

To Ginny for her long hours of labour.

To Edwina for her interest and for directing me to Hobnob Press.

To John for making it possible.

To Steve for his proof-reading skills.

To Anne for generously giving of her time in scrutinising proofs and for her helpful suggestions.

To Brigid for introducing me to Anne and for bringing me back into the life of my beloved Bemerton.

Introduction

I started these diary entries in 1936, which were chiefly concerned with birds seen in and around Bemerton. These entries expanded and evolved as I grew up. They only took place in school holidays, as I was a boarder at St Swithun's School Winchester.

~ ~ ~

During wartime service in the WRNS from August 1941 to December 1945, I recorded my diaries when on leave and on days off after night duty, when I hitchhiked home. Always preferring to spend time in the fresh air rather than catching up on sleep, I was working for most of that time at Fort Southwick (Combined Operations) deep under Portsdown Hill above Portsmouth.

In FOOT LOOSE I have made a selection of some of the more interesting entries, though at the time of writing I could never have imagined that any of it could be of any interest to anyone but me! On my marriage I placed the diaries into a drawer and duly forgot about them. Forty-five years on, I rediscovered them and they reconfirmed my deepest feeling of how much we have lost through mistreatment of the land.

The lesson to be learnt from this cannot be stressed too strongly. It is that contrary to appearances, all life forms are interconnected. Separation is an illusion. Through ignorance of this fact, we have created a sick and dying planet and a sick society, which can only be restored to Life by Love for our Creator and Love for all His creation.

~ ~ ~

I would appear to have spent the whole of the Easter holidays in 1937 birds-nesting in the water meadows! The accepted rule in those days, when birds were so plentiful, was to take no more than one egg from a nest and to take care that sitting birds did not desert. From this April my childish addiction to egg collecting gave way to observing nests, without giving their whereabouts away to roving bands of village boys.

Our garden at Bemerton was a haven for wild birds. There was a large horse chestnut in which several pairs of goldfinches nested regularly. An even taller tree, (never successfully identified) which resembled a cross between an elm and a hornbeam, was home to numerous small birds, which roosted within the enveloping ivy. Owls, jackdaws, tree-creepers and wrens nested in it. Bullfinches built in a crab apple tree and spotted flycatchers in the house creepers.

On April 1st I noted that mallards were nesting in the first field, which was in fact half an island, lying between two arms of the joint Wylye/Nadder. These ducks nested in the sedges and sometimes in the pollarded willows along the riverbanks. The olive green eggs, sometimes with just a hint of blue, were often hidden under a blanket of fleecy down, an annual wonder that never failed, set off as the nest was by the opening buds of kingcups and the delicate greening of willow wands.

Squelchy ground had to be negotiated to reach the nests. It was easy to lose a gumboot! What a stirring sight it was in the evening to watch the mallards flighting, from small groups of twos and threes to anything up to a hundred, wheeling high into the sky and then a final dizzy descent with much quacking and splashing, feet extended on to the river.

Whilst this was going on, the snipe too would be putting on their spring spectacular display, zigzagging, rising steeply in spirals, descending sharply with half open wings and out-spread tail feathers through which the vibrating rush of air created miraculous drumming sounds.

Bemerton in the 1930s was a quiet rural backwater, despite being a suburb of Salisbury. There were no more than six cars in the old village. Through traffic was mainly confined to Saturdays and consisted of hordes of taxis from Salisbury station conveying punters to the race plain. Children still played in the street at hopscotch; they whipped their tops, bowled their hoops and threw their balls against the low cob wall of Baffy Smith's cottage.

A footpath, known as 'Broken Bridges' meandered across the water meadows, alongside them and far into them. I was free to wander. Wild life abounded. Within a rectangle that lay between the village of old Bemerton, Quidhampton,

Netherhampton and West Harnham, an area approximately a mile deep and two miles long, I recorded 93 species of birds and 86 different wild flowers. Sadly today no child would be allowed to enjoy such unsupervised liberty.

The only restriction placed on me was that of punctuality at meal times and a tidy appearance for Matins on Sundays. In Bemerton we walked silently to church, three or four abreast in the middle of the street. My half sister Alison, myself and our friends, bird-nested, caught tiddlers in jam jars and crayfish and hammerheads in our cupped hands. We got wet in flooded meadows, climbed trees and canoed to distant islands. In retrospect it was sheer unadulterated bliss!

It was seeing the despoliation of these meadows and the surrounding countryside, along with a huge loss of birds and flowers, that finally aroused me to seek publication for these diaries (which had lain at the back of a cupboard for half a century). All this, not just as a sentimental recall of past glories, but in the hope that they may provide a vision and inspiration to all who truly care and work for the restoration of rural England.

Birds sighted in the Bemerton, Harnham and Netherhampton Meadows 1937-1950

Barn Owl	Dipper	Jackdaw	Nightjar
Bittern	Fieldfare	Jay	Nuthatch
Blackbird	Garden Warbler	Kestrel	Oystercatcher
Blackcap	Golden Oriole	Kingfisher	Partridge
Blackheaded Gull	Goldfinch	Lesser Spotted	Pheasant
Blue Headed Wagtail	Great Tit	Woodpecker	Pied Wagtail
Blue Tit	Great Spotted	Lesser Whitethroat	Pochard
Bullfinch	Woodpecker	Linnet	Redshank
Chaffinch	Green Plover	Little Grebe	Redwing
Chiffchaff	Greenfinch	Little Owl	Reed Bunting
Coal Tit	Greenshank	Longtail Tit	Reed Warbler
Common Sandpiper	Green Woodpecker	Mallard	Robin
Common Snipe	Grey Wagtail	Marsh Tit	Rook
Common Whitethroat	Hawfinch	Marsh Warbler	Sand Martin
Coot	Hedge Sparrow	Meadow Pippit	Sedge Warbler
Crow	Heron	Mistle Thrush	Sky Lark
Cuckoo	House Martin	Moorhen	Song Thrush
Curlew	House Sparrow	Mute Swan	Sparrow Hawk

Stock Dove | Teal | Tufted Duck | Willow Warbler
Swallow | Tree Pippet | Water Rail | Wood Pigeon
Swift | Tree Sparrow | Widgeon | Wren
Tawny Owl | Treecreeper | Willow Tip | Yellow Wagtail

Flowers found in the Bemerton, Harnham and Netherhampton Meadows 1937-1950

Agrimony
Amphibious Bistort
Amphibious Yellow
  Cress
Arrowhead
Betony
Birds Foot Trefoil
Black Bryony
Brookline
Burdock
Burr Reed
Butterburr
Buttercups (Various)
Clematis
Comfrey (purple &
  white)
Common Persicara
Cowbane
Cow Parsley
Cow Parsnip

Creeping Jenny
Creeping Yellow Cress
Cuckoo Pint
Dark Hairy Crowfoot
Flag Iris
Fleabane
Gipsywort
Globe Flowers
Great Willowherb
Greater Stitchwort
Guelder Rose
Hairy Willowherb
Hemp Agrimony
Herb Robert
Indian Balsam
Kingcups
Lady's Smock
Lesser Stitchwort
Lesser water Forget me
  not

Marsh Bedstraw
Marsh Birds Foot
  Trefoil
Marsh Cudweed
Marsh Orchises
Marsh Stitchwort
Meadow Saxifrage
Meadow Sweet
Monkey Flower
Mop Trefoil
Pepperwort
Pignut
Sweet Flowering Rush
Purple Loosestrife
Purple Milk Vetch
Ragged Robin
Red Campion
Red Clover
Small Teasel
Snakeweed Bistort

Snowdrop
Sorrel
Tufted Vetch
Valerian
Water Avens
Water Crowfoot
Water Dropwort
Water Figwort
Water Peppermint
White Bryony
White Clover
Wild Angelica
Wild Balsam
Wild Celery
Wild Roses
Wild Sweetpea
Woody Nightshade
Woundwort
Yellow Meadow
  Vetchling

1937

The Swallows and Martins are back. I watched the Sand Martins skimming the river.

I heard the first Cuckoo at 3.30am. Later on a Willow-Warbler was singing from the maple. In the meadow the ladies smock is in flower. Our big horse chestnut is in leaf; the willows and beech tree buds are bursting.

I found a Moorhen's nest with nine eggs of which three had just hatched, the fledglings were covered with black down.

There is a Moorhen's nest in the first field with six eggs so far, and a Song Thrush with five eggs in the Rectory glebe. I walked over to Wild Duck islands, Great Tits were singing. I saw the Sandpiper fly upstream, and a White Owl. At the Rectory a Mallard was sitting on eggs in a pollard willow. Another duck on the river was followed by five newly hatched young. There should have been more. Some were probably taken by pike or rats. There were Yellow and Water Wagtails about and Reed Buntings.

There was a covey or 14 Partridges in the second field, and three Reed Buntings. I found a black lizard on the cart track through the same field. There were three Water Wagtails in the garden. I watched the two cocks approach the hen with drooping wings and shuffling gait. The hen sprang at the cocks, when they came too close. They then retired to a safe distance and repeated the same procedure.

December 23

I saw a Blue Headed Wagtail on its own by the waterside. In the meadows I saw Coots and Moorhens, several Blue Tits, a huge flock of at least 100 Mallards. The drakes' heads are a brilliant emerald green. Also seen, a Kingfisher, Dab Chicks, Greenfinches. Four Swans flew over low, in musical flight.

1938

April 7

I found a Mistle Thrush's nest with eggs, in a pollard willow in the osier bed at the Harnham end of 'Broken Bridges'. Very pretty eggs, greeny grey, with brown and lilac spots and speckles. Close by was a Blackbird with newly hatched young. Ladies smock and kingcups were out and the Snipe were drumming in the evening.

April 9

I watched a pair of long-tail tits pull an old nest to bits, in order to rebuild it in a nearby thorn. I saw a Dabchick at the edge of Water Lane, also a pair of Water Rails. The Goldfinches are building in our Chestnut again.

April 26

There are a lot of baby Mallards on the river. I saw four Hawfinches in the Squarey's garden. They have big, rather clumsy looking, beaks of a grey blue colour; they whistled loudly as they shot by me. There is a Wren's nest in the ivy on one of the four willows just before Spring Bridge. The cock Reed Bunting was sitting on the low thorn bush – that is his lookout perch – looking very handsome with his black velvet cap and dazzling white cravat.

July 25

In the early evening there were ten water voles feeding on the water weeds at the Rectory. I have never seen so many together before. The meadows look quite drab from the drought. Very little loose-strife or willowherb. There is a spotted Flycatcher's nest in the virginia creeper over the drawing room window. Five dirty white eggs with little red spots and speckles.

August 30

The following birds were all bathing in the river at the same time. A pair of Yellow Wagtails, various Gold finches, Chaffinches, Linnets and Sparrows. I saw several Red Backed Shrikes (Butcher Birds) in Old Sarum Lane and a Kingfisher in Stratford Meadows.

1939

April 26

I watched a Heron flapping across the meadows. I found a Moorhen's nest and also a Mistle Thrush, and listened to a Willow Warbler singing. The Reed Warblers and Sedge Warblers are back. The Sedge never cease their singing, and carry on long after dark. I hear them from my window long after I have gone to bed.

September 12

I watched a Kingfisher sitting on the branch of a willow at Wild Duck Islands. It would fly off the branch and hover about the river for some thirty seconds, wings beating rapidly, then dive in, coming up with a silver minnow every time. The Snipe looked marvellous zig-zagging above the islands and river.

1940

April 3

I saw five Herons together in 'Para', several Redshanks, a Marsh Tit and Reed Buntings. I scared a weasel out of its wits. It was curled up asleep in an old bird's nest!!!

April 30

In the field beyond Gipsy Lane, I saw a Curlew flying around in circles crying. It perched on the wooden bridge rail, near the 'gateway to Para'.

August 27

There were 12 Herons in 'Para'. When they spotted me they flew up ponderously into the tall elms in the 'Arcadia'. I saw a Kingfisher.

October 5

I watched 7 Herons in 'Para', and managed to get up close. The willows are an autumnal mix of yellow and silver. The Swans flew overhead on musical wings. I saw the first Nightjar I have ever seen. This is not Nightjar country, and I think it should have migrated. It was lying on a single plank bridge, and I came upon it quietly and suddenly. It must have been asleep! There was no mistaking its identity. That beautiful litcheny barred plumage, and white tipped tail feathers. It flew off without a sound.

October 21

There were 15 Herons in 'Para' today. I saw a pair of Kingfishers below 14 Hatches. They whistled past me, and appeared to be chasing each other. It was a day for Woodpeckers! I saw Green, Great Spotted and two Lesser Spotted!

November 6

I saw the Nightjar again – this time lying along an oak branch.

November 27

The Nightjar is still about! This time I saw it fly out of an ash.

December 22

I watched a Treecreeper spiralling up our cedar tree, its tail spread out like a fan, a silvery grey mouse-like bird. One more sighting of the Nightjar in 'Para.'

December 27

I saw the Nightjar again in the elm tree near Cooks Farm.

1941

January 1

Metty brought the ponies to the Race Plain, and Alison and I rode with her on the down at Stratford Tony. It was sunny and frosty, with an inch or two of snow. There were flocks of Yellow Hammers on the down and Bullfinches flying about the blackthorn thickets. Also Fieldfares feeding on the haws.

January 7

There was snow in the night. In 'Para', I found tracks of Weasels, Hare and Voles, as well as innumerable bird tracks. A small flight of Teal flew over. I watched a Heron fishing in the river at Cook's Bridge. It flew off, an eel dangling from its beak. There were quite a few Widgeon at the Netherhampton end of the meadows.

March 6

I listened to Great Tits singing. The Redshanks were calling in the water meadows. I saw a Treecreeper spiralling up an old Hawthorn. Several Jays were flying around in the tops of the elms in Arcadia. To my surprise the Nightjar is still about. It was lying on a low oak bough. At my approach it flew silently into an elm. There were a lot of Wood Pigeon feeding in the fields. The white poplar at the end of the second field is weighted down with lovely big scarlet catkins, so that at a distance it looked as if it were in leaf. The Mallards were walking about in pairs.

March 13

I watched a pair of Wood Pigeon building in the cedar; they kept flying into the elm and coming back with twigs in their beaks. I found the first frogspawn by the stepping-stones, and saw the first brimstone butterfly. The bees were busy at the crocuses and the daffodils are nearly out.

March 23

The Snipe were drumming in the meadows. Walking in 'Para' I saw a Kingfisher, and the hindquarter of an otter, disappearing into some brambles. Kingcups and queen cups are coming out in the first field.

April 7

Mary, Gerald and I, decided to help the War Effort! We found an old pram and pushed it over 'Broken Bridges' to Harnham, in order to pick up tins for salvage, from the dump in the lane leading to Harnham Hill. Gerald picked up a tin and tossed it to me. Most unfortunately a Robin flew out of it and there were eggs too! Oh dear! What a bad start!

April 8

The House Martins were back at Odstock and the woods were full of primroses, violets and wood anemones. There were five Water Wagtails in the garden.

April 9

Our House Martins are back.

April 10

The Sand Martins are back, flying over the river.

April 11

The Swallows are back!

April 17

I biked over to Pitton. Violets, primroses and cowslips out. I saw two Green Woodpeckers and a Red Backed Shrike flying along a hedgerow. The larches were that wonderful rich vivid green, which lasts all too short a time.

May 1

I was out in the meadows early. I saw the White Owl at 7am and again at 11am in the little fir wood. I saw a Kingfisher near Gipsy Lane, also a pair of Redshanks. I found several nests; a Linnet's with eggs, a Moorhen with seven, a Greenfinch, quite new but no eggs yet. The alders are in leaf and there are baby ducks on the river.

May 2

The Redshanks are calling and drooping their wings in courtship flight. In the small stream in 'Para' that we call the 'River of Life' there are several quite large trout, and also dace. Three Jays were about, shrieking as is their wont. A number of Yellow Wagtails near 14 Hatches. In the first field, marsh orchids were out and water avens. In the evening at the Squarey's, I found a Hawfinches nest in the old willow at the edge of the croquet lawn. It was well hidden in the ivy and there were five eggs.

June 10

There is a Sedge Warbler's nest in the bamboos at the Squarey's with five eggs in it. Close by there is a Willow Warbler's nest with young.

July 24

I watched the Stickleback with a lovely red breast in one of the side streams in 'Para'. There were Longtail Tits in some nearby osiers and a family of young Willow Warblers were flitting about in play. The riverbanks and ditches are lush with willow herb, valerian, loosestrife and meadowsweet.

August 2

The Stickleback is still there, on guard outside its nest. As I lay across the wooden bridge to watch it, a Jay flew past me into an oak, so close that I was able to make out every marking on its plumage. I crawled within six feet of a Green Woodpecker, which was resting by the edge of the stream. When it noticed me, it screamed like a maniac and bounded off into a willow. The guelder rose berries are reddening already.

This was my last entry before I went off to join the WRNS. After initial training I was posted to Stranraer for a few months and then to Milford Haven for nine months, dealing with Atlantic convoys. Final posting to C in C Portsmouth at Fort Southwick on Portsdown Hill, a vast communications centre for Combined Ops. We worked deep under the hill, walking down hundreds of steps at the start of each shift and back up at the end. Working deep underground I became desperate for fresh air and to see the landscape and wild life. My diary continued on leaves and odd days home to Bemerton after night duty.

December 2

I saw a pair of Kingfishers in 'Para', and a large flight of Widgeon – they were quite difficult to approach without scaring. I saw the Herons, a Jay, a Green Woodpeker and two Grey Wagtails. I came very close to a weasel before it vanished into the sedge.

1942

January 12

We have had some severe frosts. The alder catkins are a wonderful deep purple. The Redshanks are feeding close to the old paper mill hatch, also a few Snipe amongst them. I was able to watch a Water Rail at very close quarters from the second iron bridge. It jerks its tails like a Moorhen and has a red beak. When it saw me observing it, it dithered and then ran past me into the sedges. There are big buds on the Black Poplars, and the hazel catkins are starting to extend.

January 15

I saw the Water Rail at the second bridge again, and I watched the Snipe feeding at the rivers edge. I saw a hare and a female Bullfinch and more Reed Bunting than is usual during the winter months.

January 16

The Water Rail was present at the bridge again. A Kingfisher was perched on a spray of brown and withered willowherb, diving for tiddlers.

February 28

The prolonged frost is holding things back. The white poplar catkins are still in small bud, and no sign of catkins on the goat willows either. The Kingfisher flashed past me piping as I walked through 'Para'; there were plenty of Snipe and Mallards to be seen, also Jays, Pigeons and a very large water rat, and a Heron. The elms are just starting to blossom and the snowdrops were out on 'The Isle of Avalon' below 14 Hatches.

April 9

Our chestnut is coming into leaf, and the willows have donned their delicate green veiling. In the meadows the kingcups are out and great patches of pink butter burr. The House and Sand Martins have returned once more. A Mistle and a Song Thrush are both sitting on eggs.

April 11

I walked to 14 Hatches and watched a Dipper perched on the only small rock above water. The herons were out frogging. The Swallows were back and Snipe were drumming overhead.

April 16

I walked through 'Para', a Jay was kicking up an awful din – quite hysterical! On investigating, I found it in the process of driving an Owl out of its nesting hole in a hollow elm. On climbing up I found the hole lined with grass, but there were no eggs. Possibly the Jay had taken them! A Kingfisher flew out of its nesting hole in the bank, and the Herons were around. The flat pink sycamore buds were spilling out of their bracts in a cascade of golden blossoms. There were pools of pinky lilac 'milkmaids' among the kingcups.

June 7

I found a Lesser Whitethroat's nest in the shrubbery, in a Cyprus tree. There were four young not yet fledged. The nest was a shallow cup, rather frail, made of grass fibres and a little hair. When worried by the approach of the cat, the parent birds scolded and churred, and made a ticking sound, at the same time darting to and fro and in and out of the bushes. In the meadows I found a Chaffinch's nest with young, and a Linnet with nearly fledged young. At the Squarey's I found a nearly completed Reed Warbler's nest in the bamboos. A pair of Redshanks are nesting in the field beyond the second field and a Plover is nesting close by. There are three eggs resting on a little straw in the shallow indent of a cow's hoof. The old birds beat around my head crying, and one feigned lame, trailing a wing to draw me away from the young. Finally it perched on a post and flapped its tail up and down in an effort too retain its balance. In Tournament Wood the broom is in flower. Its warm comforting scent filled the glades. The honeysuckle was almost out and the wild raspberry blossom.

July 4

The mimulus is out by the river. I found a Reed Bunting's nest: the young had flown. A Flycatcher has nested in the Squarey's magnolia and the young have just hatched. A Sedge Warbler's nest in the bamboos has four eggs, one of which was pure white with brown speckles.

July 6

I found a Blackcap's nest in Gipsy Lane. I can always rely on finding one there every year. It was low in the thorn hedge, interwoven with hop bine. There were four eggs, a second brood. Close by across the river, I found a couple of nests in the haystack beside the little fir wood. A Chaffinch with six eggs and a Willow Wren with four. In the afternoon I found a Wren's nest in a yew tree at the Hare warren. Coming home through 'Para' I found a Moorhen's nest with eight eggs, saw the Kingfisher, and failed to find a Yellow Wagtail's nest, despite the fact that the birds were circling round me crying! There was a big trout lurking by the second bridge.

November 25

I spotted the Dipper at 14 Hatches. Belly-crawled to the edge of the river, and watched it through binocs. It stood on a small stone, bobbing up and down, and dipping for small water fleas. It flew downstream with me in pursuit. Presently I spotted what appeared to be a white feather on a brown clod of earth. I guessed it was the Dipper, and managed to crawl quite close up to it, but keeping a clump of dead thistles between it and me. I had an excellent view of it turning over weeds and dead leaves in search of some succulent morsel. I was lucky enough to see four Kingfishers. The Widgeon are not around as yet, or more likely they are avoiding the Italian Prisoners who are cutting back the riverbanks, and rooting out the vegetation. I gave them a wide berth too! They wear brown overalls with a large yellow 'bull's eye' on their backs. A couple of soldiers were watching over them. It's said that they are very good at snaring game, to supplement their rations.

December 1

I watched a pair of Dippers below the island at 14 Hatches. They were swimming under water; they leave fewer tracks than a Water Vole, despite being so dumpy. The Widgeon are now back, though fewer than usual in number.

1943

January 21

There has been a premature feeling of spring in the air the last few days. This morning was mild and sunny and when walking through 'Para' I noticed that many of the alder catkins showed yellow pollen. The floods were out in the meadows and below the paper-mill eight Swans were feeding. There was a wonderful stillness, broken only by the occasional bomber passing overhead. I stood on Merlin's Bridge in 'Para' and watched the stream flow smoothly past the old ash tree with its mossy bole. Not a ripple on the surface of the water, except for where its flow was impeded by a brown and withered spray of willow herb, that jutted out into the water. The only colour was provided by an arch of scarlet hips that hung over the stream, contrasting with the deadness of the sedges and water plants.

There was quite a lot of birdsong at 14 Hatches from Thrushes, and Great and Blue Tits. There were half a dozen Herons feeding, and about 30 Mallard resting on the banks of the island. Returning, I caught a glimpse of reddish brown, which at first I took for a dog, but it was a fox down from the Hare Warren.

I then came across my old friend Joe Love the Carter. I hadn't seen him for ages because of the war, and him living at Donhead. He has no roof to his mouth, a cleft palate, which can make it difficult to interpret his broad Wiltshire. He says the Foxes over at Donhead are a light sandy colour, different to the norm. He gave me a lift back through the floods in his cart.

January 23

Prue came to stay, as we managed to synchronise our leave. We walked to Grovely from Ditchampton, and then parallel with the Beech Avenue, passed the fir wood to Hadden Hill. Below us lay Wishford, surrounded by floodwaters. It was good to feel the springy turf beneath our feet, and the moist ferny mosses. There was even a tantalizing smell of rising sap! The slender hazel wands had dangling catkins. The wintry sun glanced on the trunks and branches of the lichened oaks. Here and there in the sheltered coombs, grow a few solitary silver birch, and beech trees with their bronze semi-circles of fallen leaves.

In the wooded valleys the dogwood added a touch of purple to liven up the rather sombre dark green backcloth of spruce. In the glades the Great Tits played hide-and-seek among the bare branches, zit-zitting as they darted from one mossy branch to the next. The woodmen had been busy, and some of the loveliest dells were denuded of all but brown decaying bracken. The Jays were very evident, very noisy! There were roe deer about and primroses out in sheltered nooks.

February 26

I biked to Yarnbury Castle by Wishford and the Langfords. On the slopes below Grovely, I couldn't help noticing how well the tractors merged into the landscape.

They were quite swallowed up by the vast open landscape. There were large flocks of Chaffinches and Fieldfares along the hedgerows. I left my bike in Steeple Langford and walked up the cart track in glorious sunshine. At Yarnbury I perched on the old milestone. XI miles to Warminster, X miles to Sarum is still visible on its weathered surface. I noticed when passing Ditchampton that A.G. Street's autumn barley was a good five inches tall.

March 13

Our chestnut is practically in leaf, the elm brushwood is in tiny leaf, also the alders and sycamore. There are violets out along the banks of the stream in 'Para'. I waded about turning stones to look for crayfish, there were only a few small ones, and the water was very cold. I saw Herons, Jays and Kingfishers, and the Dippers at 14 Hatches I think I have found their nest under one of the hatches. In the evening, I watched the Redshanks feeding and the Snipe drumming.

March 19

I biked through Farley, Pitton and Grimstead. The larches were greening up, and primroses and violets were out in the woods and on the banks. Yellow Hammers and Chaffinches were singing. I watched a host of Coal Tits dipping ahead of me along the hedgerows. In the heart of Pitton village, Jays were very visible and vocal!

April 2

The blackthorn lies in snowdrifts along the hedgerows. I wandered over to the little fir wood to check if there were nests in the haystack, and I encountered Mr Noyce the water bailiff, and walked around with him for a while. He knows of several Duck, Pheasant and Partridge nests in the small area. There is one Partridge that is such a good mother, that he can lift her off her eggs, hold her for a moment, and on release she will settle back again without flying off! He told me that a pair of Redshanks had nested close by Spring Bridge last year, and despite the fact that boys fish and hang about there, somehow all went well. There were several stoats in the wood, and a Snipe's nest just outside, in some rushes. We spotted a pair of Long-tail tits and the beginnings of their nest in a blackthorn, and a Song Thrush sitting on eggs. In the afternoon I biked to Pepperbox Hill, where I saw a pair of Nuthatches and a Treecreeper. In the rookery the parent birds were feeding their young.

April 14

I walked around the Barford side of Grovely, coming down at Wylye. The downs were fragrant with cowslips, and charlock on the plough. Milkwort was out, its tiny flowerlets running through a range of colours; from deep blue to pale blue, pure white to an occasional rosy ink. Inside the woods, the violets were just over, but the primroses and bluebells and early spotted orchids, still delight the eye. The white beam were in full flower, and the oaks this year, seem to have jumped from the bud to full foliage without going through the amber stage. I peeked at the Blackbird's nest in the lilac. One of the four eggs had just hatched, the baby bird's beak was wide open.

May 1

I went out into the water meadow before breakfast. The Snipe were drumming overhead, and the Redshanks were dropping and calling. I found a Linnet's nest low in a hawthorn with five eggs in it. Later I biked through the Nadder Valley to Fovant and Tisbury. I stopped awhile at the stone quarry in Teffont Evias, It was worked by the Romans, though I suppose the actual hard labour was done by the Ancient Brits!

A little girl called Margaret gave me a coin she had found, saying she had plenty more at home. This one was a special coin minted to pay the army. It bore the head of Constantine, and translated from the Latin reads: 'For the glory of the army!' This I know because I took it in to show Hugh Shortt at the Museum. I came back through Chicksgrove with its wondrous Tithe Barn, and just avoided being run down by a Yankie army lorry at a narrow point. Red campions and bluebells flourish along the road verges. The most noticeable bird of the day was the Goldfinch; wherever I went, they seemed to be.

May 7

The Robin's nest in the first field was just hatching when I looked at it this evening. Some young Chaffinches had also hatched and the Linnets in the hawthorn have been out a few days. In the meads at Stratford-sub-Castle, I found nests of Mallards and Plover.

May 12

I met up with old George in the meadows. He told me about the nests he had found here, way back in 1896! I showed him the Chaffy's and Linnet's nests. The Linnets are nearly fledged now, and the baby Chaffies were grey and fluffy. 'Aye', said George. 'There be two sorts of linnet z'no, the Vuzz Linnet with the red breast and the Green Linnet (Finch)'! In those far off days, he said, he and other boys used to take a cage and place the nest in it, leaving the cage door open. The parents would feed the young, and the boys would shut the door and remove cage and young, at the moment prior to flight. Otherwise, so George claims the parents would have brought them, a 'pizen berry, and they would die'. My heart bled for them. Sounds a tall story, but George swears it's true. He says the pizen berry was that hard red lump that sometimes develops on willow leaves. He obviously believed the Lapwing and Peeweet, to be two different birds, and I didn't of course disillusion him. 'The Peeweet's egg be rounded, and the Lapwing's pointed, see!' On parting, he said, 'Master he'll laugh when I tell him I've been out nesting with a young lady! He be sure to tell my wife! But she won't mind', he assured me. His parting admonition to me, was, 'You be careful now. There be soldiers out there, and I wouldn't like you to be getting into trouble!' I promised to be careful! After leaving him, I found a hedgehog asleep under a heap of dead leaves in a hedge bottom.

May 16

The flags are out along the riverbanks. The young Blackcaps in Gipsy Lane have hatched, the Chaffies have flown, and most unfortunately the man rolling the field where the Plovers are nesting went over the eggs. The eggs were at the point of hatching, which makes it all the worse. I wish I had known he was coming. The young Linnets will fly any day now. The young Robins are black and fluffy. I forgot to mention that the Flycatchers were back on May 14. Some boys brought a young Blackbird to me, as its leg was hurt. The tarsal joint was torn and sore. I bathed it with Dettol and we fed it with a few worms. The boys will have to look after it as my leave ends tomorrow. I told them not to feed it too much at a time, and to keep it warm. This evening it is hopping about and chirruping.

June 9

I walked to Burcombe through Manor Farm and went on to Hoopside. Down below a tractor was ploughing up rough land, all thistles and poppies. I went down and asked the driver if he would teach me to plough. When he said 'Yes', I climbed up and sat over the back wheel. The tractor was a heavy International. The field had been ploughed before, during the winter in heavy rain, so the ground was very bumpy. The driver, whose name was Jim, taught me how to start up the engine, and told me to keep my eye on the wheel in order to keep the furrow straight. I managed quite well except for one crook, which he erased. He is an

Amesbury man, who has worked for Coombes for five years. He wears a white cloth cap and bib and brace dungarees. He is, I should say, about 28, though his hair is quite liberally sprinkled with grey. He is very sunburnt, and has a nice look of earth and fresh air about him. He seemed glad to have someone to talk too, as he said ploughing could be very monotonous. I gathered he is exempt from National Service because as a child, he had nearly lost a foot, after almost fatal contact with a mower. He loves everything mechanical, and knows all about machinery, having spent several years working at Bulford Camp. I thoroughly enjoyed myself, driving slowly along, slicing through and turning the earth, and watching over my shoulder the black swarm of Rooks, interspersed with a few silver Gulls as they sailed down to feast on grubs and wire worms revealed by the ploughshare.

While Jim ate his lunch, I walked over to the Ivers. At the foot of the down on some waste ground pitted with rabbit holes, I found pyramidal and military orchids, and the pretty white lesser butterfly. The latter were under a tangle of elder, thorn, nettles and briars. I climbed back on to the down through the Ivers, and ate my bread and cheese among the ladies slipper and thyme. Then I went back to ploughing. Jim flattered me by saying my ploughing was better than that of a man on the farm, who had been ploughing for over a year. I can drop by any time. On my way back over Hunt's Down the bee orchids were just beginning to open.

June 10

I walked to Grovely in search of wild strawberries. I went along the north side of the wood, till I met the track up to Hadden Hill from Wishford. I followed it into a thicket. Blue smoke was rising in a column over the oak trees, and on investigating I found two charcoal burners at work. One of them directed me to a recently felled plantation, which he said was full of wild strawberries, as indeed it was. I filled two jam jars full, which with a sprinkle of sugar, plus top of the milk. Will make us a tasty start to breakfast. The aroma is almost the best part.

Coming out of the woods on the Barford side, I met my old Woodman of yesteryear. He is 80-plus and has waxed moustaches. He said he had recognised me immediately by the way I had jumped the gate! We walked together into Wilton, where he lives alone in a little cottage, with a clipped yew at the gate. His sister comes in to see to his meals. He reads a lot and is never lonely. I remember him telling me last year how, as a little boy of seven, he had to walk from Wilton to Barford and back every day to scare birds for a farmer, and of how terrified he had been in the dark. Poor little chap, and all for about sixpence a week. That of course would have been before the 1870 Education Act. He invited me to walk home with him, and showed me his little garden. When I let him he cut me two camellias and picked me some beautiful strawberries, and invited me to come back in August for some plums!

June 11

I went to Barford to see if I could help Mr Coombes with haymaking, but he had cancelled it because of rain in the early morning. I walked over the down to Hoopside, where Jim was ploughing. He allowed me to take the tractor round on my own a couple of times. He is due for four days holiday on Monday, but thinks he will have to go haymaking instead. He is courting a WAAF but at the moment things aren't going too well and he seemed a bit out of his depth. He is very good about Plovers' nests, always keeps an eye out for them, stops the tractor, climbs down, removes the eggs, moves on, dismounts, scoops a hollow in the earth with his boot, replaces the eggs and moves on. The old bird comes back and settles down.

These three days in the open air have been good. I have lost the look of mushroom pallor from the tunnel, and am nicely sunburnt on the face and neck. On my way home I jumped down a bank, just missing landing on top of a Yankee Corporal, or whatever they call themselves. He was sitting in the long grass about Burcombe Manor Farm. I don't know which of us was the most startled. Our resultant conversation was hardly brilliant. 'Hallo! Where are you going to?' 'Home'. 'Been picking flowers?'. 'No ploughing'. 'With a horse?' 'No tractor'. 'Wal Wal, can you stay a bit?' 'Sorry I have four miles to walk. Goodbye'. Poor chap. I expect he was lonely.

September 15

It has been a sunny but chilly day, and the first time I have been home for some time. I biked to Burcombe, and walked over to Hoopside. As usual Jim was ploughing. He seemed pleased at my unexpected appearance. It breaks the monotony to have someone to chat to. Since I hadn't looked by since July, he hadn't expected to see me again. I explained about the ten-mile limit on travel for service personnel, which had now been lifted.

On Hoopside a man was trapping rabbits among the elder clumps, and Farmer Coombes and a shooting party passed in open line across our furrows. Also the Home Guard were out on manoeuvres so there was plenty to watch. Jim seems fed up with ploughing and talks of going to work in an aircraft factory. My guess is he won't leave. He started ploughing out a fresh piece of land, keeping in line with a mark at the base of the Ivers; its marvellous to see how straight he keeps over such a vast expanse of ground. As I was leaving, Mr Coombes came over and warned me not to go through the charlock, or I might get shot!

October 12

I biked to Fovant. There was a thick mist, which clung to the folds of the down and only began to lift around midday. I climbed up to Fovant Hut on the old coach road. (It is of course much older than a coach road, being an ancient trackway). I ate my sandwiches between Chislebury and Boxbury. These two great shoulders of downland, surge above the plough. A few small coveys of Partridges about, but only five or seven in each.

November 8

I managed to hitch an army lorry going to Shaston and they dropped me off at Arundells. One of the soldiers gave me a Swiss Roll – very nice, as I hadn't brought a sandwich! I climbed up on to the old coachway running roughly from Sarum to Shaston. It is rather a grim approach, the rugged shoulders of down kept reminding me of a ruined Norman keep. There was a good stiff breeze and a clear view away to Shaston, Cranborne Chase and the Ridgeway.

There were men burning gorse bushes and ploughing up the virgin down on either side of the track. I came down between Fovant and Compton. Because of the firing, the red flags were up beside the track. In Burcombe I managed to get a bus. It was very crowded and I didn't get a seat until Wilton. The man in front of me turned round and to my surprise it was Jim. He told me he had been married for three weeks to his old flame the WAAF, after re-meeting her at 'a hop' in Amesbury. I am very pleased. I had a feeling that he would do so in the end. Mr Coombes has given him a cottage near the farm. We had a brief but pleasant chat and then I got off at Skew Bridge.

1944

March 29

There are at least two Mallards' nests in the first field. One is under an old hen run, the other among the withies. My eye was caught by the rusty red breast of the drake, through a small gap in the sedges. The Sand Martins are back. Nine of them were joyously circling the river, in company with three Swallows.

May 18

I shouldn't be home, but here I am! I came home by the back streets of Salisbury to dodge the Military Police. (The 10-mile travel limit was in force with the build up to D-day) I found the Redshanks nest in the usual place. The Plovers were calling anxiously, and I saw two youngsters couching in the slot of a cows hoof. I picked one up. It never stirred, just moved its head slightly once. There was a Linnet's nest in a guelder rose.

1945

March 14

Spring is backward, the chestnut buds hardly showing white. I walked the length of the Coach road and back, about 20 miles in all. I saw the first Wheatear on Hunt's Down, and a large Buzzard with a huge wingspan. There were more Wheatears about on Hoopside, where I saw a stoat run down a bury. In the beeches above Bishopstone there was great activity in the rookery; so many hungry mouths being crammed!

April 15

I looked for Plovers' nests in Stratford Meadows. I failed to find any, but I flushed a Snipe from four mottled brown eggs in a cow's footprint, which was lined with dry grass. It was very hot and sunny. The chestnuts proudly bear their conical white and pink blossoms, and the lilacs are out. President Roosevelt was buried today. God help the new man, he will need it.

May 21

I started off to go nesting, over 'Broken Bridges' when I fell in with four village boys. Gordon Stanley 14, Hugh Taylor 13, another lad of similar age, and their little hanger-on, Dickie Adams, a merry little brown faced varmint of nine. They asked if they could come with me, if they promised not to touch the eggs! So off we went!

Gordon waxed enthusiastically about my supposed prowess. 'She can climb better than any boy and find more nests.' I just hoped I could live up to this unexpected and exaggerated tribute. Then he asked was it true that I had caught a German prisoner? This astounded me, 'Who ever told you that one'. I asked. Came a chorus: 'Your sister did Miss!' 'Then she was pulling your legs' 'Well,' said Gordon, 'I didn't think a girl could do that!' Hopefully adding, 'Could you?' I said I thought it rather unlikely, adding tongue in cheek, that if I came up behind one, and caught him by surprise, I could try out my Ju Jitsu! There was an awed silence, while they considered this, then he said, 'I won't half tell your sister off!'

By now we were near the haystack. 'Lets go and look at it,' I said. 'There are usually a few in there.' There was a Blackbird and a Willow Wren. We crossed Spring Bridge and turned off for Gipsy Lane, where there was a Blackcap sitting. Hugh started talking in a La-di-da manner, doubtless imitating me. 'Where did you get your feened accent from?' 'What's a feened accent?' said little Dickie. 'Oh! All la-di-da' said Hugh. They all laughed. 'People with feened accents are usually very nice,' said Gordon, adding rather surprisingly. 'They're not snobs!' 'You must be strong to be in the Navy, Miss. They only take strong people!' Here followed much praise of naval discipline, gleaned from fathers and elder brothers. They did not think much of the Yanks, who pinched their brother's girls!

I pointed out a Thrush's nest. A parent bird was perched above it with a worm. Coming back by the Plover field we found a rat had been at the Redshank's eggs. A Moorhen shot out from some rushes. Dickie found the nest. There was a mad scramble as they all went for it! No power on earth will keep boys off Moorghies' eggs. I didn't try. Each boy took two, I made them each put one back. Gordon tore his trousers on some barbed wire, diving under it. He was going to hide them from 'Mam' in his bottom drawer. I took him home with me, and patched them. I hope they passed muster.

In the evening I swam in the rain at Wild Duck Islands with Alison. She flatly denied the German Prisoner story!

June 22

A glorious sunny day, not too hot. I biked up Roman Road, and on to the Turnpike. On the corner, where it joins the avenue from Wilton, was a wondrous sight! A large field, pure white, not a blade of grass showing! For one moment I thought, 'snow'. It looked so natural, and here and there were drifts where it seemed deeper. It was of course an amazing spread of oxeye daisies!

Beyond that the Plain was predominately yellow from mustard or charlock.

It scented the breeze and appealed to the eye, but I think the scent is not to every one's liking. Away to the left was Grovely, and beyond it the Great Ridge. I coasted down Camp Hill into the Woodford Valley and made for Normanton, where I left my bike. The Plovers wheeled and screamed around me as I climbed the down. I went through a gate and along by a line of firs. A few Turtle Doves flew out of them and went along in front of me, flirting their beautiful white-banded tails.

Straight ahead of me was Long Barrow Crossroads, and the string of road barrows near Diment's. Stonehenge looked strangely black, surrounded by deep cloud shadow, while everywhere else was bathed in sunshine; for a fleeting moment it seemed to resemble some Egyptian temple gateway. Such a pity that Larkhill has spread out such ugly tentacles towards it, in a great sprawl of crude red brick. From one angle it seemed as if Stonehenge was in line with the limits of the camp. Before turning back I took a last look. It had turned to a ghostly white, and this time all around was shadow.

I went back over Wilsford Down, passing a haystack where a tramp reposed in blissful slumber. Then on down a slope where yearlings were grazing and up again over the sheep-cropped turf. The milkwort a little over, but there was still spikey leafed squinancywort, with its tiny pink and white clustered florets and there were masses of red winged dwarf orchids, with their curiously pungent smell. The deep red of the calyx gives them a smouldering look, like that of a small poker. I lay on a small barrow and surveyed the sky, and breathed deeply of the pure air, and all the time the Plovers cried around me. I ate my lunch and watched the bees as they visited the orchids and a team of horses ploughing up the opposite downland.

I came down by Lake House, and talked to a wounded sailor who was convalescing at Wilsford Manor. He had been a survivor of the Royal Oak. I turned off into the Avon Water Meadows, spotted a willow with a low branch overhanging the water, and contemplated sitting on it and dangling my feet in the water. Just in time I spied the approach of a fisherman, so I beat a hasty retreat to a small stream I sat on a broken hatch and looked into the water, pulled a leaf off a yellow globe flower and the oxygen bubbles streamed up to the surface. Quite fascinating. I biked back by lovely West Amesbury, and home by Stonehenge and Longbarrow.

June 23

I was up early and off to 'Para' to bathe in the 'River of Life'. The mist was curling up off the water. The stream was dredged recently by the Italian Prisoners of War and now flows quite swiftly. I left my clothes under the solitary ash tree on the bank that we call the 'Tree of Life'. While I swam about, a Green Woodpecker was breakfasting on ants. Such a long mobile tongue!

September 13

Alison, the two Reynolds girls, and myself, went to the Great Ridge. We were lucky with our hitches. We took the track up from Chicklade into the woods. Harvesting was going on, later up here than with us. We walked round a field of red clover, and made for Pertwood and its little Norman Church, half hidden by tall nettles and surrounded by beech trees. We ate lunch on the edge of the wood and watched the wild life around us, which consisted of a solitary stoat, a couple of racing deer, several grey squirrels, two Lesser Spotted Woodpeckers, a Nuthatch, and some Coal Tits on the thistles.

Walking down Well Bottom, the down on either side was a hazy blue from devil's bit scabious. A tractor driver gave us a lift on his trailer, and we came out between Corton and Tytherington, and caught a lift home from Heytesbury.

1946

May 29

Oak Apple Day [celebrated at Great Wishford in connection with rights of common in nearby Grovely Wood]. I was up at 5am and biked in soft sunlight to Quidhampton. White strands of mist lay across the meadows. Here June joined me and we went on through Wilton and along under the tall elms to Wishford. Several gardens already had oak branches waiting to be erected on the houses. Going up the track to Ibsbury was a bit like meeting Burnham Wood coming to Dunsinane! Coming towards us were elderly women, men and children, all carrying their oaken bough. There was a very thick dew and the grass was soaking. We entered the wood through the little wicket gate. The bluebells were over, but there was plenty of wood sanicle, red campion, and a few lesser butterfly orchids. There was a strong smell of herbs, calamint and wood sage. The hazels had been stripped naked by caterpillars. When we came down the hill, an oak branch had been fixed to the church tower, and the bells were ringing out. We met the Rector making his way belatedly to the wood.

OAK APPLE DAY

I was young a little mad, and filled with the magic of May,

When I rode up to Grovely at first faint flush of day.

For I was one with the wind and sun,

The stable earth, all good deeds done,

A part of the Spirit Eternal

There as I rode passed bush and tree.

The hidden rides of inmost Grovely hock high in fern,

A glimpse of blue, a flash of red,

Two screaming jays flew on ahead

In raucous harmony.

Archangel and Moschatel, tiny Woodruff steeped in dew,

Canopy of hawthorned May and Bluebells hyacinthine hue,

All reflected that diurnal morn

When the joyous sons of Heaven

Shouted as the skies were riven,

'All glory be to Him!'

Exulting with trysagion

For all is finished all in One

Then I left the choir supernal

For the earthbound and the vernal,

Cuckoo, Wood Lark, Willow Wren.

Mist like milk filled hollows in the downs,

The church emerging while the village drowns,

Jacobs's sheep dissolve and disappear,

Shift sideways, vanish, neither here nor there,

Frangible illusion.

Suddenly there I was among

A host of folk both old and young

Waving green boughs.

Their's annually to bear and take;

To deck their doors and merry-make,

Shout 'Grovely and all Grovely'

J.E.H. 1946

June 7

At the Squarey's there is a young Cuckoo, fully fledged, in a Reed Warbler's nest in the bamboos by the river. The foster parents were very fussy and protective of it, busily stuffing the ever-open beak of the voracious alien

August 6

Bank Holiday – my last free day before starting work at Petersfinger Farm tomorrow. June and I hitched to Tinhead on the northern edge of the Plain, via Tilshead and West Lavington. We began by climbing Edington Hill. From the top there is such a contrast between the great rolling plain, with its ripening grain, and glaring chalk tracks, all ending quite suddenly in a scarp. And beyond it, bathed in a blue haze, are the flat, lush green fields, edged with a tall elms, stretching away to Melksham and Chippenham.

We could pick out Steeple Ashton Church. The surrounding countryside was once very much into cheese production, and of course Steeple Ashton was an important centre for wool distribution. It was a very hot, sultry day, and we were glad to emerge on to the level ground near Tinhead farm buildings, which were deserted. There were notices everywhere warning: DANGER KEEP OUT. UNEXPLODED BOMBS, SHELLS, etc. I think we were crazy, we didn't seem the least bit concerned, merely changed direction, and headed south, hoping to hit the Sarum-Warminster road, and keeping an eye out for shells!

The down was rough and unkempt, but florally rich with field scabious, knapweed, devils bit and frog orchids. Then we hit traces of a track, which I had a feeling would bring us to Imber. We followed it across a wasteland, and what happened next was quite weird and had a *déjà vu* quality about it. It was like being in a dream.

We came into Imber past the deserted Manor House and into the dusty street. The cottages were blasted, the windows gone, and an awful stillness pervaded every corner. It was a sorrowful place. Near the church, a man and two women holding flowers stood beside a car, waiting to enter the church (which had not been a target for shells). Although I had never seen any of them before, I knew the man, and exactly what he was going to say before he opened his mouth. He said, 'Have you a pass? You shouldn't be here without one!' I said, 'No, we came here by mistake.' He said, 'Two Army men are on patrol in a car. They'll take you to Warminster if they find you.' We said we would walk on towards Warminster. 'Well, whatever you do don't go off the road. There's any amount of live ammunition around!

Walking out of Imber was like walking a cross a battlefield, the road was shell scarred. Blasted trees, gaunt black and tortured spectres devoid of life, uttered a silent scream at their desecration. We passed a gutted barn, and a couple of miles on, some soldiers were filling in holes in the road. At one point a Little Owl appeared from nowhere, and flew on ahead of us towards Warminster. We passed those two mighty earthworks, Scratchbury and Battlesbury, and entered the town without mishap. Next day the *Daily Telegraph* printed an article on how after all these war years, Imber had been opened up for the day to former inhabitants!

Petersfinger

I first met 'The Boss' in 1943, when hitchhiking home from Fort Southwick. I was standing at Brickworth, where the Southampton-Romsey roads converged, hoping for a lift on to Salisbury. Traffic, what with petrol rationing, plus it being Sunday, was minimal. The Boss was returning from harvesting at Titchbourne. He stopped and gave me a lift and I recall him switching off his engine as we glided slowly from the top of Pepperbox Hill to The Three Crowns, about a mile downhill. I told him that I wanted to farm after the war, and since I was on a week's leave, he invited me to help with the harvesting the following day. From that time on I managed to hitch a lift from him again on several occasions. Eventually I took up an offer made by him to come as a student to Petersfinger.

On August 12 1946, I presented myself at Petersfinger Farm, situated on the Southampton-Salisbury road, a mile outside the City boundary in the southeast corner of Wilts. The name derived from the fields having once been let out annually on St Peter ad Vincula's day. The farm consisted of low-lying water meadows, which stretched to the banks of the River Avon opposite the village of Britford. It was a haven for wild life. The old brick farmhouse abutted the road on a very awkward bend.

According to my whim or the weather, I either cycled there daily from Bemerton village, or was picked up by The Boss or Fred the Dairyman, when they delivered the milk churns to the small depot in Ashfield Road at 8am in an old truck lorry. As a student I received no pay, being liable initially to be more hindrance than help. On the plus side I received a very good meal with the family, and the occasional gift of a rabbit. Students at Pete's were willing dogsbodies, only too willing to prove ourselves however heavy or dirty the work.

There was a milking herd of thirty or forty non-pedigree Shorthorns. Several of the best milkers were 'blue' (Shorthorn-Friesian cross). Unless the weather was exceptionally severe they wintered out at night. During the winter months they fed on hay, silage and chopped mangolds, supplemented with dredge corn and a little concentrate for the high yielders. The dredge corn was freshly ground daily, which was quite a laborious process, requiring two people, one to feed the grinder, the other to turn the handle.

Half a mile from the farm was 'Rangers', a large field shaped like an isosceles triangle. In the winter of 1946-7 it was divided into stands of marrow stem kale, mangolds and swedes. The point of the angle ran out at Queen's Manor, an ancient farmhouse on the Clarendon Estate.

Titchbourne was five miles from Petersfinger and stood on high ground. It could be approached from the base of Whiteparish Hill at Brickworth by a footpath across fields and through a copse, where a hurdle maker often worked. Going by road and taking the right hand fork, one came to the tiny hamlet of Harestock, where another right turn took one to the red tiled farmhouse.

At Petersfinger the dramatis personae were: The Boss, his schoolboy son Robin, Fred the Dairyman, the Landgirl Pat, with occasional help with haymaking and harvest from the Boss's daughters. Fred and Pat worked together and were rather aloof from the rest of us, their work revolving around the dairy herd. Another Landgirl, Rosemary, did all jobs as required. Carter Symes was over 70. He looked after the horses, Smiler and Pleasant, and did hedge trimming and water meadow work, mangold pecking, and much spreading. He lived in a small brick and flint thatched cottage on the farm. His son, Walt, was foreman He lived at, and looked after Titchbourne, along with his wife and youngest son, Doug, who did most of the tractor work. Finally there was 'old George' who lived in a thatched cottage at Harestock near Titchbourne and did casual work when required. Joining the farm later as students were Lizzie aged 19 and Paddy 15.

My physique was very slight, and until I developed skill and muscle, the daily work was very hard indeed. But after three years of working underground — at Fort Southwick in the WRNS — I was thankful to be out in the open air.

August 12

On my arrival at Pete's (Petersfinger Farm), I was given a hook and sent to chop thistles in the orchard, with a warning 'to watch out for my legs'. Beyond the orchard is a low wooden cabin, where Fred lives with his wife and an aloof Landgirl called Pat. It rained all last night, but the morning sun shone out fitfully. At 11am I was sent to help load up wet grass on to the wagons with Carter and Robin. We put several loads for silage. A strong gale got up, interspersed with heavy showers, and I had not handled a prong before, so my efforts were pretty ineffective and my breath came in heaving pants.

After the grass had been loaded on to the wagon, it was taken to the silo, which resembled a small concrete tower, for unloading. There it was straightened out and trampled down. Carter allowed me to drive Smiler back to the silo with the last load, through the water splash. Carter was very nice to me in a gentle jokey way. He told me he had come to Wiltshire from Dorset in 1914. After lunch I worked on the silo with Rosemary. She has an attic room in the farmhouse and works terribly hard, rising before 5am to help Fred get the cows in for the morning milking. She is rosy cheeked and has light brown curly hair. She told me she had been brought up in an orphanage, and on leaving it had joined the Land Army. A life of hard toil is what she has been led to expect and she seems to accept it more cheerfully.

August 13

While the wheat was being cut at Titchbourne this morning, Mary and I were driven over in the truck lorry by The Boss and sent to cut bracken with George. Later we were set to work hiling oats at Studland. After lunch The Boss came back, and we all went to hile the 14 acres of wheat in front of Hangall's Copse. By 4pm the last strip of wheat dwindled in front of the reaper and binder, and as the last ears fell, five rabbits bolted for the open, hotly pursued by the excited dogs, men and girls. A most welcome addition to the meat ration!

All this took place against a backcloth of untamed, natural beauty, several miles from the main road. There is a sunken way behind the wheat field, in which wild marjoram and canterbury bells run riot, a pageant of purple and mauve, while the reddening berries of the wayfaring trees fringe the edge of the copse. A final touch to the scene is given by the pink tufts of hemp agrimony, which attract the butterflies that bejewel each fluorescence, in particular the peacocks, five to one flower head.

That same night (I wrote in retrospect, after several weeks with no daily entry) the rain fell heavily, and subsequently harvest became a grim business, quite a feat of endurance. In the few fine intervals we cut and hiled and tried to carry. Too often after reaping and binding, the rain came down in torrents and it became impossible to continue working. Hiles were left where they fell, to be picked up later, sodden and twice the weight to handle. Thus it continued, week in and week out. It was heartbreaking to watch as the wheat and oats began to sprout in the hile, for lack of a chance to dry out. First a fine network of white filaments covered the ears, followed by green sprouts in the outer hiles under the shadow of the hedge.

Because of the uncertain weather we worked fast and furiously, in an effort to get the hiles on to the wagons, and off again on to the ricks before the next downpour. I had to acquire the knack of remaining upright, as the wagon creaked and groaned its way over the undulating ground like a sailing ship in motion, and all the time sheaves were coming up at the loaders without pause, and from every direction.

I found it a relief occasionally to be asked to drive the Fordson along the hiles, even though it was sometimes difficult to make out instructions against the throbbing of the engine, the youthful profanities of The Boss's son, and an occasional lapse into broadest Wilts from Walt. September came and the evenings shortened and grew chilly. In spite of double summertime still being operational as during the War, it was often dark as we threw off the last load, and the stars shone out as we drove homewards along the deserted lanes.

September 16

After days of enforced idleness as regards harvesting, The Boss decided that, fit or not, the dredge corn must be carried! (Dredge corn was a mixture of corn and peas that had been grown in the war years to supplement the cattle feed in winter). Mary and I started throwing down the hiles at the top of the field, and Walt started doing likewise at the far end of the field. Suddenly I heard him yell my name. 'See here Jane!' I raced down the slope toward him. He pulled aside a hile and there nestling under the butt was a neat round nest of rabbit fur, warm, and plucked from the breast of the doe. Burrowing into it I found three young rabbits, not more than two days old. Together we moved them into the shelter of the long grass beneath a thorn. (I wish I could say that the doe returned to them, but we did not return to Hangall's again until the rick was threshed the following January.) Our worst disaster has been the peas, which were grown for canning. We had 17 acres of dwarf peas on a very open, exposed piece of ground. They were beaten flat by the wind and rain, and Walt had to cut them by hand. The majority were black and charred-looking. Many had spilled from the pods and the remainder were badly discoloured. When we came to pick these peas, we disturbed large colonies of shrews that fled in all directions emitting high-pitched shrieks. I found a nest of 12 fat velvety babies, one of which had a white star on the nape of its neck. How I would have loved to have reared them, but being insect eaters they need to eat voraciously in order to maintain their body weight, so it would not have been possible. Late in the afternoon it came on to rain heavily again, and we had to pack it in.

September 20

Temporarily defeated by the weather, we have retreated from Titch's to 'Pete's' and, probably in desperation to give us something to do, The Boss sent Mary and I to dig up 'pinkies' in 'Oak Tree' with Carter. 'Pinkies' are clumps of coarse wiry grass. We were equipped with rounded spades that had been well sharpened. Several good steady heaves at the base of the pinky and it came away cleanly since they are shallow rooted. We then threw the pinkies into a putt cart pulled by Pleasant and later they were taken back to the farm for burning.

'Oak Tree' is a water meadow, so-called since it has one oak tree roughly in the centre. While we were working there, we saw a pair of Green Sandpipers, they are larger than the common sandpiper and have white tail coverts and green legs and feet. They are passage migrants. We flushed them out of a ditch from which they rose with a cry of 'kit kit'. In the late afternoon a White Owl cruised low along the hedgerow coming within a few yards, then suddenly becoming aware of me, it gave vent to a startled 'Eek', and did a smart right turn away.

During this period Mary and I have picked apples for storage from trees in the young orchard on the southeast side of the house. There were many varieties of cookers and eaters. We picked them by the bushel, carried them into the house, and finally staggered with them up a ladder leading through a trapdoor into a dark airy loft under the rafters. We laid the apples out on the shelves, taking our time over this, and, without invitation to do so, we sampled and enjoyed as we worked! It seemed a just reward for our toil.

Some afternoons I help with the hand milking, tying up and washing down the cows muddy teats and udders with warm water and disinfectant as they come in from the wet meadows. At first I was given a few old cows that were nearly dry to practise on. Later, as I became more proficient and the milk began to flow with a satisfying ping into the pail and it was seen that I was not ruining the cow's udder by straining at the teats, I was trusted with the milking of freshly calved cows. Eventually I became a quick milker, handy with a hoe and good on the rick. The skill of which I was most proud, was loading a wagon, placing each sheaf correctly so that the load did not list to one side.

October 1

We finished harvesting. The rakings were carted this morning! The last rick went up at Titchbourne on September 28. We spent the afternoon scything thistles in Skillery. Harvest was really over and we were relieved and thankful. Thankful that there would be no more endless plodding up and down and round the fields, picking up the sodden hiles that had been thrown down to dry in the rare sunny intervals between the showers. We were weary with being soaked to the skin, having our wrists and ankles chafed and our discomfort compounded by the thistles in the outer hiles. Even so, compared with other parts of the country, and even with neighbouring farms, we had come off lightly. This was because of the high ground on which Titchbourne stood and its soil, loam over chalk. We were spared the dispiriting experience of seeing the blackened heads of our hiles emerging from flooded fields.

Throughout this dismal harvest The Boss continued to be his usual imperturbable, unflappable self. (He was at that time I suppose about 50). A small dapper man with a trim moustache and dark brown hair greying at the sides, he was quietly spoken and quick in his movements, and was never without his pipe. He was always smart, even in old clothes. His gaiters, polished till they shone, reflected the puddles as he strode through the farmyard. Every day he would walk round the farm, on the old principle that the Master's foot was the best dung! He could appear suddenly as from nowhere, keeping his workers on their toes. I don't recall him doing much heavy work, probably because he had problems with his back. He had been injured in the First World War, when as a young airman he had been shot down. He had regular treatment for this, from a remarkable old lady from Basset, in Southampton. She was an amalgam of herbalist, osteopath, and white witch. A rare person to find in those days when Medical Science held all the answers and the healing arts of our ancestors were dismissed by all but 'cranks' as so much superstitious nonsense and quackery.

The lady's name was Mrs Swinbourne. She was deaf and reminded me of a gipsy queen. Her manner was warm and dignified. She dressed in many diaphanous garments, and round her neck as well as necklaces, she wore the cumbersome deaf aid box of the time. She arrived at the farmhouse most Saturday afternoons, an upright figure sitting in the back of her chauffeur-driven Daimler.

As it turned out it was very fortunate for me that she did so for, but for her, I believe I should have lost the use of my hands and arms. In the early days of harvesting, I noticed that the tip of an index finger was numb, as if, as I thought, a prickle were in it. At first I ignored it, but then I found that all my fingers and thumbs, and presently my hands were similarly affected. The numbness was bad, waking me every few minutes at night, and my hands felt like swollen balloons. This made difficulties at work. Milking became painful, as my fingers were stiff and hard to bend. Lifting became a penance as electric shocks ran up my arms. Dr Gubbins came to see me and was plainly baffled, suggesting aspirin to help me sleep. I took a week off work, but it made no difference and when I found I could no longer open doors or knit in the evenings, I was alarmed.

At this point The Boss came to my aid, suggesting I saw Mrs Swinbourne at the weekend, at the same time warning me that it would be painful. But it was well worth it, as from the first visit my hands began to improve. Mrs Swinbourne listened attentively as I spoke into her microphone, her beads, mostly jet, jangling alarmingly as she leant forward and intoned, 'You, my dear, have blocked nerve centres from nervous tension.' We traced it back to the War. 'If you had not come to see me', she said, 'You would have lost the use of your hands.'

I lay down on a sofa and she plunged her right hand into my solar plexus, kneading it like dough, stopping at intervals to give me a chance to recover from the pain. Next she worked on my spine and neck and finally up my arms with a twisting movement that released a series of electric shocks. I visited her for several months and each night found me soaking my arms for ten minutes in hot water and mustard powder, deep enough to cover the elbows. Then it was a quick leap into bed to keep the hands warm. Under the bedclothes I rubbed Vic into each finger and wiggled them hard for ten minutes – surprisingly hard work. When the numbness had receded and the pins and needles gone, under Mrs Swinbourne's instruction I gathered an armful of comfrey from the meadows, boiled it up and spread the resulting goo on bandages which were would round my arms at night to strengthen the arms and nerves. A messy business but it did the trick.

On the farm we swung into a winter routine that centred round the well-being of the cows. Their comfort and feed were paramount. First came 'mucking out', a daily affair, and as winter came on the volume and quantity of dung to be removed increased. First the cowshed: here all dung and straw had to be brushed into the gutter, which ran the length of the house. Next the contents of the gutter were swept up into manageable heaps for forking and shovelling into the barrow. Then the barrow was trundled across the yard and on to the dung heap. The calf pens and bull were cleaned and bedded down. This left the cowshed to be sluiced with buckets of water, followed by lots of vigorous brush work with the yard broom, a good way to warm up on a cold day. Finally the concrete strips around the out-buildings were swept clean. The centre of the yard was a slough into which it was unwise to venture, and which at the end of my time was concreted over. Some days I cleaned up on my own, sometimes with Mary. Later Lizzie and I worked together. At first I could not manage a full barrow load, and the empty shovel weighed a ton. With time, however, full loads were no problem, and a thankless task could be exhilarating.

October 16

For the last few days Mary and I have been 'drowning' in the meadows with Carter. (Drowning was the art of Water Meadow management, and the man in charge was known as the Drowner). At 'Pete's there was no longer a drowner and such work as was necessary to prevent the main ditches from silting up was done by Carter and us. The meadows are criss-crossed with ditches and wooden hatches (a few still in use), which had once controlled the water flow. It had once been traditional to flood the meadows in winter, in order to produce an early bite for the cows. The banks had not been cut out for some time. We had to slice through them with special rounded spades, and then the mud was hauled out with gravels (clawlike forks). This was surprisingly heavy work, and our feet were often wet and cold. Since the meadows teem with wild life, there are always diversions of one sort or another. Green Woodpeckers are frequently seen and today, hearing an excited chattering from a mixed mob of rooks and daws, I looked up and saw a Heron in the midst of them, being chivvied along. It appeared quite unconcerned, and minutes later we witnessed a repeat performance.

In late October we pulled mangolds at 'Rangers'. Due to the compaction of the ground by so much heavy rain, they were hard to pull up. Mangolds are pulled with the left hand and at the moment of lifting the tops are sliced off with a hook and roots and leaves are dropped in separate heaps. Mary, Pat, and I each worked three rows at a time, the whole action acquiring a rhythm of its own. I soon became very quick at this, ending up ten heaps ahead of Mary. At the end of the day we covered up the heaps of mangolds with the leaves against the frost. First thing in the morning we would walk to 'Rangers' to cut a stint of kale; later Carter would come with a horse and waggon that we would help to load. The kale stems were glazed with frost, particularly after rain, followed by freeze-up, when the stems appear to be coated in 'glass'. It was hard on the fingers, and as the sun rose and the thaw set in, the wet leaves soaked and drenched the sleeves of our coats. When the cows are bought in and tied up for milking, I go with Fred to help throw off the kale from the wagon, around the field where the cows are overnighting.

November 5

The Boss was very rough today, so Fred came out to the depot with the churns. I joined him and we drove straight to 'Titch'. The trees were a beautiful sight and apart from the ashes, which were bare, all appeared as leafy as in June but the most wonderful colours. The hazels were still green, the ground ash and oaks a mixture of green, gold and brown, the hedge maples lemon and pink, the dogwoods purple, while the beeches were a blending of bronze and yellow. While we waited for the threshing gang to arrive, I joined Carter and George spreading dung, flinging it straight to the ground from the cart.

After ten minutes we heard the sound of the threshing machine and the big orange box came into view drawn by the steam engine. On first sight the gang seemed a rough lot and thoroughly disagreeable. The air was filled with oaths and everything was 'bloody'. George was sent to build the straw rick, with myself and

John (one of old Freddie's men) helping us. Walt had been sent drilling, and this was unfortunate for the rest of us as the elevator was set at a roaring pace. It was sheer hell! By 3 pm I wondered if I could stick the afternoon out John kept murmuring about slave labour and wouldn't move round the rick so that he was more hindrance than help. George's clothes were wet with sweat. At last Walt joined up. 'Poor old Jane!' said he. 'Are you tired?' 'A bit,' I said, which was an understatement. At the end of the day the yield from eight and a half acres was 85 sacks.

November 7

We were threshing again, this time dredge corn. Thankfully Walt was in charge of the strawlift, so it was set at a sensible rate and was child's play after yesterday! George and I built the straw rick. I overheard Hubie, one of the threshing gang, say to Walt, 'I reckon that girl's a brick, or she'd never have stuck it yesterday.' Quite an accolade!

We all had lunch (dinner!) with the Symes. Mrs Symes, a very nice person, rosy-cheeked and buxom, she is perhaps, 42 or 43. You feel that she is really good, which goes for the whole family as well. It shines out of their eyes. She, Walt and Doug, live in the old tiled farmhouse. No comforts, no electricity. All water pumped from the well. The food dished up was stodgy and the pastry heavy. I was glad not to have to eat it!. The men tucked in with keen enjoyment, to rabbit stew with mountains of potatoes, followed by apple pie.

The men sat on wooden chairs at the scrubbed wooden table in their shirtsleeves and black waistcoats. George, with his beautiful white hair and rosy cheeks, sipped tea from a saucer. Walt, lithe and handsome, with glossy black hair, ate off the blade of his knife with a simple dignity. You would never have taken him for the father of married sons. Doug, the youngest son is 18, the tractor driver. Smiling, friendly, rosy-cheeked, his appearance just spoiled by bad teeth. He is courting the girl in the mauve dress, who makes tea for lorry drivers in the tin shack cafe on Pepperbox Hill. Carter, the grandfather, was born in Dorset. He is of the ancient British type, small and dark, unlike the large boned, fair, flaxen strain still sometimes seen in Wilts. The talk at table was mainly about darts. Both Walt and Doug play for the Fountain Team at Whiteparish, Walt being the leading hand. Mary and I ate our cheese sandwiches, and we were pressed to have pie, which we refused!

November 8

Over to 'Titch' again for more threshing. George and I were on the straw rick, and again a gale was blowing. We finished the wheat first, and had just started on the dredge corn, around 3:30pm when the gale reached near hurricane force, and the men were saying that no-one, but 'Mad John' (as the head of the gang is aptly named) would attempt to thresh in such weather! Hubie, dark haired and doe-eyed, twice slipped me an apple, and Carter stuffed me with choc, 'to keep your strength up', which it did very nicely! The straw was blowing off the rick, over the hedge, into our faces, and down our necks, so it was pretty foul going. Afterwards George and Hubie weighed me on the weigher. 'Seven stone?' asked Hubie. 'Eight,' said I, 'Quite right, well done', said he.

November 11

The Boss and I drove over to Titchbourne. We dressed the seed corn in the old barn with a pink powder called Agrosan G. The barn, a wooden one, stands on staddle stones, their purpose being to keep the rats out. Old George and I turned the corn in the churn all morning, while Walt and Doug went drilling. Talking of Mary who has just let the farm, George said: 'She were a nice little girl, but too meek hearted. She would rather cry than quarrel!'

November 18

Typical day for the time of year, boring routine. I clean up the cow pens and wheel out the muck, clear up the yard, clear out and litter down the bull and calves. Then I walked over to Rangers and joined Fred who was cutting kale. Later we carted it to Skillery, ready for the cows after milking. In the afternoon I milked ten cows, and ditto for the rest of the week, managing eleven on Friday. The Boss bought an 11-month-old half-pedigree Shorthorn bull for 52 guineas. It was a nice looking beast with wide horns.

December 20

I saw my first Bittern today! Sadly it was a dead one. Shot by the Boss's son in Long Meadow. He having mistaken it for a Heron. It upset me badly. Oh, why must some men shoot everything that moves? Bitterns are such rare visitors to Wessex. I examined the bird at close quarters, and saw the preening comb. (The middle toe is indented after the manner of a file) It was a most beautiful bird with mottled chestnut plumage, and olive green beak and legs. The Boss presented me with one severed foot!

'The Gateway to Paradise'

Alison reading the Beano on the hatch over the River of Life, 2 May 1941

Snow in *Arcadia*, 7 January 1941

I spotted a Dipper at 14 Hatches, 25 November 1942

Heath Hill and Grovely Woods, 23 January 1943

Hoopside and Burcombe Ivers, 9 June 1943

View from Spring Bridge to Gipsy Lane, 21 May 1944

Cathedral from Spring Bridge, 21 May 1944

Oak Apple Day, Grovely, with early morning mist, 29 May 1946

'Hammersmith', Great Ridge, 14 April 1946

Bemerton Rectory: the river and view of 'First Field', 11 June 1947

The rather boring road to the Great Ridge Wood, 22 May 1947

Lifting *spuds at* Titchbourne, 21 July 1947

Ashcombe and Wingreen, 11 September 1947

Lifting spuds at Titchbourne, 21 July 1947

Brixton Deverill Church from Riversdale, 10 September 1947

1947

January

The New Year started mild, sunny even at times with a hint of warmth, with larks singing overhead as we cut the last of the kale at Rangers. Ornithologically it has been an interesting month. On Jan 4 the first of the Tufted Duck appeared on the gravel pits below Milford. Curiously, they all appeared to be drakes. They were joined a week later by Pochards. The Coots and Moorhens, who are the permanent residents, did not appear to resent the intruders! A Grey Wagtail took to visiting the farmyard. Huge murmurations of Starlings passed from the direction of Stratford sub Castle and flew towards Harnham Hill, a little before 8am each morning. I would see them flying back at about 4:30 pm. Another Bittern was spotted at the gravel pits. One morning, while driving Smiler and Pleasant round Long Meadow, I saw a Little Owl sitting on a willow branch.

January 20

Elizabeth arrived at the farm today, as a student. She was at the Godolphin School with my half-sister Alison. A pleasant, competent little girl, with rosy cheeks, brown, lustrous eyes, a tip-tilted nose and a roly-poly figure. She is quite mad about horses. We went muck spreading together at Rangers. We are now giving the cows chopped mangolds in the crib at milking time, as it is too wet in the fields. The cows were also getting hay and crushed oats, with a little cake. Fred cuts great flaps of hay daily from the rick. It looks an arduous task. There is a surprising amount of bird song for the time of year. Song Thrush, Chaffinch, and Great Tits, all singing lustily. Fred the taciturn, not given to praise, told me that my milking was up to standard!

January 24

Winter has come! The hard frosts have frozen the neat hummocks of dung that we had thrown out on to the fields from the putt cart into solid immovability, making muck spreading into a laborious process of bash and scatter! Carter would pause, lean on his fourgrain and say with his usual twinkle, 'Spread it even now, so it don't grumble!'

A few more nights of hard frost and we were forced to abandon muck spreading, for nothing short of a pneumatic drill would have done the job. The cold was so intense that the cows' breath froze, and they came in for milking with icicles hanging from their nostrils, so that they resembled walruses! The only time I felt really warm was sitting up against the cow milking, and this despite wearing three and four jumpers under my jacket. Morning jobs after mucking out and washing down were in short supply. The Boss would send Lizzie and I off with billhooks to chop back blackthorn, not easy, since our hands were too cold to grip the billhooks. On one such bitter morning, a very old tramp and his wife set up a rough bivouac in a corner of the hedge, just inside Oak Tree, and there they overnighted. I felt so sorry for them.

January 27

More snow after severe frost. I was lucky enough to see another Green Sandpiper in Long Meadow, down by the Bourne. The snow was wonderfully thick and dry. I plunged a hand and arm into it and came out bone dry.

February 1

There are Fieldfare in great flocks feeding on the remaining hawthorn berries in Skillery. More indiscriminate shooting! The Boss's friend shot a strange bird in Lambsbury, in mistake for a Snipe. Opinions differed as to its identity. The Boss took it for a Dunlin. Mr Pitman (a local birdman) thought it might be a spotted Redshank, a rare passage migrant, while I thought he was probably right. I looked it up in my Coward's. It definitely resembled a Redshank but the legs were orange.

February 19

At last, the strange bird has been identified as a Redshank in winter plumage! This day is the twenty-seventh day of hard frost. For the first time in 14 days, the sun came out for a few minutes at 4pm. So many grey days prove very depressing. One never feels warm, possibly because rationing means we have insufficient fat in our diet. In Lambsbury where the ground is still slightly soggy, I noticed many more Snipe than usual feeding. The Starlings that used to fly over from Stratford in December at 8am and back at 4:30 pm were now leaving at 7:30am and returning at 5.00pm. Several panels were removed from the silo, and Fred now has the added task of cutting out the silage, which is a rich treacly brown in texture a bit like a heavy pudding. It has a far reaching odour, spicy and pungent, that lingers on the air and clings to the clothing with the persistence of dung. It had in fact been doused with molasses at intervals, during the preparation of the heap. This was supposed to assist in the 'cooking' process, and to make the silage more palatable. Certainly the cows relish it!

Carter remarked that over at Titchbourne, the foxes and Magpies were so hungry that they were taking the rabbits from Walt's traps. Lizzie and I now take turns at mangold grinding, one tipping the mangolds into the machine, the other turning the cold, iron handle. Then we carry the fruits of our labours along the back of the cow pens to tip the cribs. We spend a lot of time clearing up and loading silage on to the trolley, off-loading it again by the cowpens.

February 22

There was another fall of snow in the night, and I notice that large flocks of Yellowhammers come daily looking for food in and around the silo.

February 24

The hardest frost yet, really bitter! We went over to Titchbourne to thresh oats. 'Mad John' had bought a bailer this time. I was on the rick with Hubie, and an unknown chap was feeding the drum feeder. When I climbed on to the rick, I was blue with cold. Within half an hour we were all roasting, and cast off our coats. Had there been a river to hand I would happily have jumped in! At half time I changed places with Liz, and threaded wires through the bailer, opposite Ernie Rowde. Hundreds of baby field mice fled from the rick as the bales were flung off. Some of the outer bales were frozen in, and took a bit of shifting. We ate our lunch in the shelter of the rick, in bright sunshine, all very pleasant. Afterwards I went on wiring with Ernie, while Walt weighed the sacks and loaded the trailer. Doug and the unknown chap drove the sacks to the barn, George and Lizzie were clearing cavan and Carter made the bale rick.

February 25

Today was even colder! Lizzie had asthma caused by the dusty cavings and was absent. I was on the bailer with Ernie. We got on famously, he being quite a card. He is dark and slightly saturnine and wears a cap. He has very amusing eyes, and every time they caught mine, I had to smile. We had short bursts of chat between threading the wires. During the War, he was in the Military Police at Deal, and I was intrigued to learn that he had been at Fort Southwick. Before the War, he had shown horses and carts at Wiltshire Fairs, and acted as a jeweller's carrier. At a guess he is about 45-50 years old. 'Mad John', he said, had got him out of the

Military Police after five years service. I was rather embarrassed when he suddenly remarked, 'You don't come from the working people!' This was so totally unexpected, that I feebly said, 'What do you mean? ', which was pretty dopey! 'You don't come from the working class?' Uncertain how to handle this, I said, 'How do you know?' The obvious answer came, 'I can tell from the way you talk!' 'Well then I don't. Class is rather horrid.' 'Yes, but I didn't know how else to put it.' Ernie didn't care much for threshing, (Well, it can hardly be many people's favourite job!) but he said that the pay was good. On parting at the end of the afternoon, he remarked that he would miss me tomorrow, and my beautiful eyes, and smile over the bailer! To which I replied, 'You'll be quite happy with the other land girls.' 'No! They won't be like you.' He wasn't being flirtatious and it wasn't banter. I felt he meant it quite sincerely. Later on he said that he supposed my being in the Services had made me broadminded, that I would make a good farmer's wife, and that he would be glad to work for me if I farmed in the area.

The gang are moving on in the morning, but will be back later. I said goodbye to Ernie, adding that I hoped to have his company then. On weighing up we had taken 136 sacks of dredge corn, 13 sacks to the acre. A good sample but some of the peas were black. Yesterday's were goodish, considering the weather. There was some discolouration, but The Boss was pleased since they were off the worst land on the farm. I noticed that the clover opposite Clapgates appears to have vanished. (It had flowered last summer, and was due for a top dressing).

I had to rush from work on my bike as I had an appointment with Hickman (my dentist). With no time to wash or change, I was dusty from head to foot from cavan. The receptionist looked aghast, really horrified! But Hickers took it in his stride, and didn't bat an eyelash merely remarking as he worked the chair with his good foot, 'I've never seen such a dirty little girl in my life!' Luckily, since he also farms, he was amused.

March 4

Still no let up from the weather, it rained heavily all day, followed at night by a frost, which froze on the trees, glazing the trunks and branches, so that they seemed sheathed in diamond veils. A lovely sight, and when the wind got up the branches tinkled. It continued alternately raining and freezing for several days with the same magical effect. Each blade of grass was coated in glass and knobbly to walk upon.

March 5

This was the worst night of all for the cows, because of the rain, which froze as it fell. The branches of the frozen trees creaked and groaned in an extraordinary manner. Here near Salisbury there is not much snow, but Fovant was cut off, the top road to Amesbury was impassable, and telegraph wires were down on Pepperbox. Not a sign yet of Rooks building in the elms in The Close.

March 11

The thaw has come, pouring rain and the Avon has flooded the meadows.

March 12

The cows slept in for the first time this winter because of the flooding. Contrary to what one might suppose, cows prefer to be out whatever the weather. Bring them in and the milk yield drops, quite dramatically.

By mid March, the mangolds from Rangers had given out, and Doug had to come all the way from 'Titch' with a trailer load, through torrents of rain, with a sack over his head. We were all fed up with such a relentless, long drawn-out spell of 'caddling' weather. One day wet, the next, frost and snow, and icy roads, and by way of variation we had a tremendous gale on the 16th but the following day was bliss. Warm sunshine and midges hovering around the dung heaps. Signs of better days to come!

April 1

I saw the first Swallow on the wall of the house, as I biked off to work. When I arrived at 'Pete's, Redshanks were flying around the meadows with quivering wings, ascending and descending, in nuptial flight, and giving vent to repetitive musical outpourings as they did so. Spring, though long delayed is on its way! The Boss, Lizzie and I set off straight away for Titchbourne, leaving Fred, Pat and Carter with the cows. Half the threshing gang had turned up so that we could bale hay from the rick. I came to the conclusion that they weren't such a bad lot as they had appeared back in the autumn; obviously it had been a particularly bad day for them!

By the middle of the week, all the silage and mangolds were finished, and the cows are again out at night, but they are restless, knowing that by now they should be out at grass. They were off their feed and looking scruffy! We watched the first House Martins circling the yard.

April 9

A lovely soft, sunny day, so wonderful after what we have been through. Lizzie and I were sent to Oak Tree to pull up wild onions, 'So it shan't taint the milk,' as Carter put it. A pointless and dispiriting job. There was so much of it! The elms at last are 'pinking up', a couple of months late.

April 11

Walt was sowing oats at 'Titch'. I stood behind on the cultivator and worked the levers. A wonderful hot day, you could see all the moisture being drawn up out of the soil, in a shimmering haze. Outside the copses, the banks were a mass of white violets and primroses.

April 14

My half-sister Alison and I decided to hitchhike to Shearwater on the Longleat Estate. Petrol being still in short supply the roads were wonderfully traffic free, each village cocooned in a peaceful self-contained isolation.

When hitching there is always a frisson of excitement. Will we eventually make the place we are aiming to reach? How many cars or lorries will pass us in the hour? Will any of them stop? Or be going in our direction? Will we end up having to walk back, possibly in the dark? Well, today, we picked up a lorry in Wilton, and it dropped us in Stapleford. We walked slowly on along the road admiring the delicate green veiling just beginning to hide the bare limbs of the willow trees in he water meadow on the one hand, and enjoying the enthusiasm of the choir of Larks, as they rose and fell above the down on the other.

We had just reached Little Bathampton, when the first car stopped beside us, and a rather shy youngish man asked if we would like a lift? We started talking about the Great Ridge Wood, a favourite haunt of ours, and discovered that he farmed at Stockton. I boldly asked him, 'Are you Frank Sykes, author of *This Farming Business*? 'Yes,' he blushingly replied, 'had I read it? And what did I think of it?' My turn to blush as I confessed I had found it all a bit too much for me! The place dear to his heart was Tytherington Hill. He said he had ploughed it, but had spared the ancient village site. The ruined house at 'Hammersmith' is on his land. An ugly square brick house, miles from any village. It stands under a solitary sycamore tree, at a point where many old trackways meet in a deep and desolate bottom, quite swallowed up by the Plain, lost in the folds of the downs. It could only have been built for a shepherd, and I thought it must have been abandoned but no, it was used by the Army for target practice! He told us that the War Department wanted to take over the Great Ridge Wood permanently. We expressed our horror, and he went on to say that he thought the War Ag [*War Agricultural Committee*] had prevented it. I do hope that may be so.

The Great Ridge Wood is seven miles long, and it runs along the top of a ridge of chalk downland. The ridge itself extends as far as Wilton, and it is crowned by yet another ancient forest, Grovely Woods. Through the centre of both runs a roman road. The Ridge itself divides the Wylye and Nadder valleys.

After saying farewell to Mr Sykes, we hitched a ride from a lorry going to Crockerton. A piece of luck, since this was likely to have proved the most traffic free part of our route! From there, it was but a step to Shearwater. The peaceful lake with its gently rippled waters, and ruined boathouse, nestled against a background of rhododendrons, firs and fine beech trees. The first little brown Sand Martins, newly arrived, were skimming the surface, their snowy breasts almost touching the water, and a few Great Crested Grebes swam about in a desultory manner.

About a mile beyond the lake, along the lane, are four aged ash trees gone 'Arthur Rackham'. Their once pollarded contorted trunks bulging grotesquely, their dropping branches curling fantastically, resembling gnarled and bony goblin's fingers! Eerie at dusk! It turned wet, and we were lucky to hail an ancient lorry, that had seen better days! We sat aloft in the open back enjoying the magnificent sweep of downland (only partially obscured by rain) along the Deverill Valley and the slow winding descent into Mere, passing Celtic fields and hill forts, which quite suddenly gave way to the tamer landscapes of the Blackmore Vale.

May 8

The hot weather continues. Doug came over to drill kale and mangolds at Rangers. I walked behind to watch for the drill not flowing as it should. The heat was oppressive. After finishing work at Petersfinger I went off nesting in the water meadows, and then biked along the back lane to Burcombe. I left my bike in the old chalk pit and climbed the track that leads to Hoopside. There, on the slope of the down, under a group of old and twisted thorns, I watched three little fox cubs playing outside their earth. They were boxing each other and tumbling down the bank under a canopy of blackthorn blossom (very late flowering because of the long winter). I have never seen it more spectacular! Where the down and plough land merged, there was a yellow tide of cowslips and oxlips.

May 9

I was again sent over to Rangers, this time to cut the bank. Doug was also there, harrowing with the Fordson. After a while, he kindly asked if I would like to switch jobs. Nice for me! In the afternoon we threshed wheat at Hangalls. I was on the straw rick with George and Lizzie. At first it was very sultry, but several heavy showers left the air much cooler. There were any amount of rats and house mice in the rick. Hubie found a nest with twenty-four babies.

May 10

A perfect day. I biked to Swallowcliffe, left the bike and climbed up to Castle Rings to see the bluebells. The sight surpassed my expectations! Banks and ditches were a solid sheet of blue. Their scent hung on the air. Here and there were embellishments, clumps of primroses, wood sorrel, and that tiny curiosity called moschatel or town hall clock. There were five different species of ferns, some growing from the branches of the mossy trunked trees. One old oak had a fine honeysuckle winding its way to the top. The ground ash and hazels on the outer ramparts were being felled, and my two favourite beeches (giants of their species) had the red spot painted on them (indicating that they would soon be cut down) but for the moment they look sublime, with bluebells and ferns springing from their mossy roots. I sat awhile and watched the Blue Tits performing acrobatics on the hazel wands.

May 12

In the evening I walked in the meadows. The Swifts were flying low over the grass. A Wood Pigeon sat tight on her twiggy nest in a hawthorn, for once she did not clatter off, but eyed me watchfully with her beautiful gold-rimmed eyes and soft pink-feathered breast. I found a Moorhen's nest in the forked branch of a willow that rested on a pile of waterweed on top of the water. In it were five spotted eggs. It won't stay 'unragged' for long, it's on the village boys beat, and Morgies eggs (as they call them) are an irresistible attraction to them.

May 13

I left my bike at 14 Hatches, and searched what I call the blank fields for nests, for blank they are, year after year, though I once found a Goldcrest's nest suspended from a spray of ivy hanging from a willow. The thick water herbage, and rushes, looks an ideal site for Reed Buntings and Sedge and Reed Warblers. In the line of grey pollard willows, parallel with the park wall, the bees were busy; the air was filled with their humming. I like to imagine Sir Phillip Sidney walking in these meadows and composing his Arcadia, but more than likely it was within the Park Wall barely a stone's throw from where I stood.

May 15

I looked at the Whitethroat's nest again in the evening. The hen slipped off quietly without a sound. Despite the growth of foliage, I could just make out a slate grey head and white throat. A few yards further on, in a hawthorn, at about shoulder height, I found a Sedge Warbler's nest, neatly made out of dry grass, and just a little moss, and two pieces of white wool as ornament! Five days later the hen started incubating four eggs. She has a very distinct white eye-stripe, but I can no longer make it out because of the intervening foliage, so I stayed close by and saw the hen slip off. Her mate joined her and they 'churred' for a bit, so I moved on.

May 22

Alison and I hitched to Codford, and walked along the flat rather boring stretch of road to where it ends. Then three tracks fan out and ascend the Ridge. Along the boring bit, which nonetheless has a superb view of the wooded heights, Corn Buntings perched along the barbed-wire fence that runs beside the road, wheezing and jangling monotonously.

Inside the wood the bluebells stretched as far as I could see, among the dwarf lichened oaks. On the wide grassy ride that is the Roman road, they were an iridescent carpet of blue and mauve, shot with pink. There were masses of yellow archangel, bugle and wild strawberry blossoms. On the down, cowslips and orchids. Alison and I picked posies of wood violets and ate our sandwiches at the foot of an old oak tree. In the glade Whitethroats sang around us, and there was an occasional burst of 'jug jug' followed by that liquid crescendo of music from a Nightingale. 'Bliss was it on that day to be alive!'

Leaving the wood we came down at Chicklade, and a short hitch took us to the Stockton end of the wood. Sitting on the down, we watched a Buzzard circling round above a small thicket of thorn and elder. Presently another joined it and they flew round and round in gradually heightening circles, like giant moths. Afterwards I found their nest in the thicket: there were no eggs. Close by we found two Magpie's nests and a Chaffinch. Alison saw a large dog fox, and we found a pretty little hairstreak butterfly, with green undersides to its wings.

May 24

It was terrifically hot. Sweat ran in rivers down my forehead and nose while milking the cows. Crouched on a milking stool, right up against the cow, is like being pressed against a hot radiator. An awful thing happened during milking; Fred stripped Bridget behind me, and I had left two pounds in her. I was shaken! Quite a smack in the eye! I had thought I was getting to be a good milker. Bridget is a brute to milk, she tends to hold on to it. She had been giving 15 pounds at afternoon milking, but on the last recording day I put her down for 11-and-a-half pounds. Quite a drop!

May 26

I went back to Stockton Down and found the fox's earth with droppings and a hare's foot outside, and a great spire of yellow mullion by the entrance. Round about, where the cubs play, the grass was flattened. I noticed a sheepdog rounding up cattle, and presently the drover came over and spoke to me. After a cheery 'Good morning' – he went on to say, 'Sure I thought it was a fairy sitting there! – 'No doubt as to the land of his birth!' He works for Frank Sykes, and I guess goes home to Ireland to spend his pay. There was no sign of the Buzzards.

May 31

A broiling hot day. Liz and I were sent round to Rangers to move kale stumps to the far end of the field and burn them. Quite awful in the heat! I cooled off in the evening, swimming in the river at the Squareys's. Masses of fluffy willow cotton from the catkins were floating downstream. The Swans with five little signets swam by and on seeing me all the little ones scrambled to safety on to their mothers back! The cob bringing up the rear, eyed me distastefully as I trod water, hissed, and sailed majestically on.

June 1

Carter came with Lizzie and myself over to Rangers. We were hoeing between the new drills of young kale in blistering sun at the Queens Manor end of the field. The Turtle Doves were crooning in the overhanging elms, and occasionally they would fly down for dust baths and flirt their white-banded tails. No need for a watch at Rangers. We tell the time by the trains going to and from Southampton, high on the embankment above Gipsy Lane. Sometimes Carter will pull a watch from his pocket to check for punctuality. 'There goes the eleven twenty, right on time.' When the twelve fifty sped on its way to Sarum, it was time to knock off and walk back to 'Pete's' for lunch.

June 3

The temperature reached 95 degrees today. The sweat dropped unhygenically into the buckets along with the milk. It was hell! As I milked, I visualised the delight of swimming in an ice-cold river as soon as I got back home!

June 4

I helped Doug unload dung at Rangers and in between loads I hoed mangolds with Carter and Liz, spaced out one behind the other in our separate rows. The ground was very weedy with lots of creeping buttercup and couch. Over at 'Titch', they were very busy with both tractors, Allis Chalmere and Fordson, ploughing at Hangalls. Three cultivations, it was then rolled twice, chain harrowed and rolled again before sowing mangolds.

The following week it was mostly haymaking, interspersed with mangold pecking in the morning, whilst the wakes dried out or were turned by Carter with the side delivery rake. There was trouble with the 'fly' and Liz and I were given an apparatus a bit like that which is used for marking tennis courts. This was pushed along the drills leaving a trail of white flea beetle dust behind it, and hopefully deterring the little black hoppers.

'The 'Vly' be on the Turmut,' the marching song of the Wiltshire regiment, became a rallying call most mornings. Mangold pecking meant bunching small clumps at hoe distance. Later the clumps are singled, and even seconded to make sure the spacing is correct.

June 9

I walked to Burcombe Ivers, to see if the butterfly orchids were out, and there they were, among the brambles and thorns, at the foot of the Ivers. The scent quite delicious! How lovely they would look in a bridal crown. Many of the orchids were 18 inches high. Moths pollinate them. Baby rabbits were darting in and out of the thorn and elder clumps on Hoopside, and fragrant and palmate orchids were out.

June 11

After a day spent mangold pecking and milking at Petersfinger, I looked in on the village fete on the rectory lawn, and did a bit of gardening. After supper I biked over to Lake, along the Woodford Valley. Everywhere haymaking was in progress. It looked good, and smelt good. On Lake Down, rabbits were everywhere, I sat on the old ditches; there were orchids wherever I chose to look, pyramidal, fragrant and dwarf winged burnt tipped, which really do smoulder! The sheep have not run in the bottom this year, and the grass is tall and flower filled with reddening sorrel, oxeye daisies, and my favourite dropwort, its crimson tipped buds bursting into creamy bloom. Also pink sanfoin, tiny blue and white milkwort, (once used in cheese making) and the yellow and red of 'eggs and bacon' as my nanny used to call bird's foot trefoil.

June 13

After singling mangolds in the morning, I was hay making at 'Titch' after lunch. It was a good thick cut, mostly rye grass and red clover. It was nice and cool on the rick with George, Walt and Fred, who had left Pat and Liz to see to the milking. An unknown man was feeding the elevator and the Boss was sweeping with the car. It was pleasant and easy going. At 7:30 it rained and we had to stop with only half-an-hour's work left. We finished it the following day and Bowman the Keeper came up and gave us a hand.

June 17

Mr Chapman (the birdman) was anxious to see a fox's earth, with a view to photographing it. Diana Dunn picked him up, and then me, and I showed them the one on Stockton Down. He placed a strand of cotton across the entrance to make sure it was inhabited, which of course it is. We saw the Buzzards being mobbed again, this time by Jackdaws. A solitary lesser butterfly orchid was growing beside a clump of dyers' greenweed.

June 28

Haymaking in Long Meadow. Good, sweet, meadow hay, full of herbs. Lizzie and I pooked all afternoon, rolling up the wakes with our prongs, into manageable heaps for easy pitching on to the wagons. Carter harnessed up the horses and we spent the whole afternoon loading. In the evening Lizzie and I helped Fred on the rick.

June 29

(Sunday) Ernie Rowde asked me over to tea with his family, at Nomansland, beyond Landford. Quite a long bike ride, with the two long hauls up Alderbury Hill and Pepperbox. Ernie met me at the Landford fork. His wife had laid on a sumptuous tea, and is a nice genuine country woman. Also present were two grown up daughters and a boyfriend, Ron, who is batman to the general at Tilshead. Also the two youngest daughters, Sybil and Hazel, aged eleven and eight. Nice mannered little girls, in pretty cotton dresses.

    After we had eaten we walked in the Forest, ending up at The Lamb for a shandy. Ernie biked back with me as far as Brickworth, and at the silver fir junction, we passed George, all dressed up in his Sunday suit, just off to the Fountain! I expected to be ragged next day but he obviously hadn't recognised me in my glamorous buttercup yellow dress!

July 4

It has been one of those dull days, when rain seemed imminent all day. The Boss was anxious to make an early start picking up the hay in Skillery, but it was late afternoon before it was fit to carry. After clearing up, I went singling with George and Liz, and later Doug joined us, after bringing round a trailer-load of dung. I milked in the early afternoon, and then poked hay, until teatime with the Boss and family. Everyone turned out to load the hay and I worked on the rick until 8:15. We just finished in time before the rain came. I hear that between Oxford and Lincoln the corn is in a bad way and hardly worth the harvesting. Locally, so far, the crops look very promising. Cincinnatus, in the Farmer's Weekly, commented that in driving through Wiltshire, he had seen haymaking in progress as late as 7:00 pm. We could show him something.

July 7

A new girl arrived at the farm today. Paddy, only 15, but bigger than Liz and looking all of 22! She joined us for mucking out. That done, we traipsed over to Rangers to hoe swedes. A much easier job than with the mangolds, because they were at the clean end of the field. No suffocating weeds to contend with! Paddy was full of chatter, wanting to know if I had lots of boyfriends and when I told her I had been in the WRNS she said, 'But you are still awfully young aren't you!' I assured her I was. Bless her heart!

That evening after work, I biked to Lywood's with Liz. She keeps her ponies there. She rode Fingal, a Connemara, and gave me Dusty, a beauty of 15 hands, improved New Forest, and very well schooled. Liz thought I controlled him very well, and she said that some people could not manage him at all. We set off along the green lane to Homington, passing the gipsies, who were spaced out, higgledy-piggledy fashion. Tethered ponies, dogs, and 'tattered young'. Much whinnying, barking, and, 'tell your fortunes ladies.' We passed unscathed! We made for the great yews, passing Tozer's curious Longhorned cattle. Towards Blandford the sky looked ominously black and stormy and the wind was wild. Damerham Knoll stood out most dramatically. Round the Grims Dyke that skirts the northern edge of the yews, were masses of marble white butterflies. The dark yews looked as remote and solitary as they must have done when the sheep-stealers sought refuge there.

We did a long round, going as far as Studland, before turning back. We passed the lonely cottage in the copse. The old woman who lives there, with her daughter and mentally retarded grandson, came to the door to see us. It must be rare for anybody but the Keeper to pass their way. It is more primitive and isolated than 'Titch'. Sometimes, when hay making or threshing, we would see the three of them pass, the child running ahead as they crossed the fields, to catch the Salisbury bus at Brickworth. Gossip said that the child's father was a Yankee G.I.

July 12

At 'Pete's' the farmyard is being concreted, so no more cesspit in the middle. Just in time for the arrival of the milking machine. Whilst it was being installed, I loaded dung with George, who told me more of his life story. His father was a small farmer who could not read or write. In some way, his older brother had taken advantage of his father, financially probably. Anyway, George at 16 ran away from home with a friend. They walked from Wareham to Bristol, begging their way, and then from Bristol to South Wales.

July 15

St. Swithun's Day, and very hot and thundery. We finished the hay in Skillery and started lifting in Oak Tree (two of the fields). I milked in the afternoon, and now manage 17 or 18 cows with the machine. Would the wild onion in the hay taint the milk, we wondered? Fred, Pat and I, threw off a load of hay before tea. Afterwards we all pooked in Oak Tree until 6pm. Then it was back to the dutch barn, where we were crawling around bent double. It wasn't possible to stand upright, and the heat and dust was worse than the 'Black Hole of Calcutta'. I was in the middle, as Paddy cannot manage yet, and Liz was whacked, and the dust must have been bad for her asthma. After dealing with three loads, with sweat dripping in my eyes, plus the choking dust and heat, I was ready to drop. The crossbeams were in the way for passing and we were all doubled up. Lizzie and Paddy then tried to do it between them, but in the end we all stood in the middle. Despite the hellishness, there was terrific banter going on between George and us. I just managed to catch the 8:15 bus into Salisbury.

July 17

I woke at 2:15am, dressed and crept downstairs and out through the dining room window, preceded by Hamish the ginger tom, which slunk off into the night on some errand of his own. All sound was magnified by the stillness. My footsteps crunched loudly on the gravel drive. It was one of those summer nights with no darkness in it. As I crossed the first big footbridge into the meadows, a large white Swan passed under it, and loomed out of the night with a hiss. I watched as her brood of eight cygnets followed her under and downstream. There was a thin line of light over Harnham Hill chalk pit; the moon tried to break through but the grey cloud closed over it again like curtains. I crossed the big wooden bridge by the old paper mill, and went into the second field. A breeze arose and stirred the sedges into sound. The meadowsweet and oxeye daisies showed up white and blobby. There was an occasional 'quack' from a Mallard in the reed beds, and the distinctive 'plop' of a Water Vole. An hour later the Moorhens were out foraging in the half-light of early dawn. At this time they venture far from the riverbanks, to places they avoid in the daytime.

July 19

I had agreed to participate in the Natural History Society's 'Hawk Count' on the Plain. Each of us covering different sections. My allotted portion was to be from Stapleford, covering Berwick Down over to Yarnbury Castle, across Maddington Down, ending up at Orcheston St George churchyard, where we all had to converge by 4:30pm. I left my bike in the Castle Ring near the farm at Stapleford, and started off along the old trackway, making a wide sweep of Berwick Down and visiting all the little beech covers, where the old turf was pitted with rabbit holes. There was a lot of gromwell growing by them, with its peculiarly hard flinty seeds. There was plenty of Wheatears bobbing around in the ant heaps, and a few Stonechats. It was hot with heat haze. The usual sheep were on Cow Down, newly shorn and gleaming white. Flying low and feeding between them was an attendant flock of Starlings. Marble whites (butterflies) were everywhere, and the track was ablaze with ragwort, knapweed, and oxeye daisies.

Once I had reached Yarnbury, I stayed there an hour, ate my lunch and walked the outer ramparts, which are about a mile round. Yarnbury always surprises me: until you have climbed the first rampart it looks pretty inconspicuous. It is an Iron Age fort with three ditches, and is a wonderful vantage point overlooking many miles of plain. Until the middle of last century, hiring fairs were held there annually. Farmers would go there to hire farm servants for the year. Each man or woman seeking employment would carry the emblem of their trade: a shepherd his crook and a hank of wool, the dairymaid a milking stool.

Hawks were conspicuous by their absence, not so much as a Kestrel in sight! Leaving Yarnbury, I took the right-hand fork, just past the old milestone. On my left side, 80 acres of Cocksfoot had been cut and hiled, and beyond, another fine crop was being mown. From beside an old rusted plough on the verge, I put up a covey of ten young Partridges. More Wheatears, Corn Buntings and Stockdoves were everywhere, but no Hawks! After I had crossed Maddington Down, I went straight to Orcheston Church to wait for the others. I was out from 11:30am to 4:30pm. Normally I would have expected to see at least four or five Hawks.

I lay in the long grass near the grave of one Job Gibbs, and read *Eothen*. On a ledge above a church window a Flycatcher had built a nest. As the parent birds flew back and forth with flies, I caught a glimpse of the gaping crimson throats of the voracious young. The others doing the count drifted in, and incredibly not one Hawk had been seen by any of us! I walked back by Chitterne Barn, near which I had heard that Quail had been sighted. I did in fact hear them, but did not get a sighting.

July 20

Alison and I biked to George Fox-Grant's new farm near Rockbourne. We walked his 700 acres, some of it very poor ground, on an exposed piece of downland, but a belt of trees shelters the farm buildings. The old Cranbourne-Sarum road runs through his land. There are some grand expansive views over to Vanity, the Great Yews, Gallows Hill and Damerham Knoll. George was dowsing for water for his cattle. He cut a forked spindle twig for each of us, and we all walked earnestly back and forth. Great excitement when our twigs were pulled downward by an irresistible force. We all confirmed each other, and we could all dowse! The site of water was on a typical poor scrubby piece of ground, near some blackthorn on Blackhill.

We went back to the farmhouse for a splendid tea, laid on by George's mother and aunt. Afterwards we asked our aunts, who had known the family in Ireland, how it was that George, whose mother spoke with impeccable cut-glass tones, had managed to acquire such an interesting and unique mix of Dublin brogue overlaid by broad Wiltshire! Evidently as a small boy, he had picked up the former from his nanny and servants. It was considered at the time quite deplorable that his parents had allowed it! Then on moving to Wilts, and being too delicate to be sent away to school, he quite naturally acquired the other. Rather fun we thought, most original!

July 21

We all went over to harvest the early potatoes, (Eclipse) in Hangall's; that included Carter and George. Walt used the spinner, and Doug was digging. It rained most of the time, but we carried on. We finished the following afternoon. It was warm and sunny.

I stayed on and had tea with Walt and Doug, and afterwards Walt gave me a lesson in pulling straw for thatch. He is such a good craftsman, with an artist's pride in his work. His tidy pyramids of straw bundles, (elums) moved like a poem. He showed me how to pull the straw out, and then twist it into a rope, while pulling the loose end under the left foot. You then place the first elum, and the second goes slightly let to right on top of it, while the third goes on right to left. The wild canterbury bells and marjoram were out in the hedgerows amongst the bracken. I walked back to the road through Bats Croft, to catch the Salisbury bus. On the high ground by the croft, it was so clear that I could see the ships in the Solent.

While we were working, Walt told me about his early life. He started as under-shepherd on a 1000-acre farm in Dorset. Later the flock had to be destroyed because of Foot and Mouth, and the old shepherd was so heart-broken that he died, just like one of the shepherds in Hudson's *A Shepherd's Life*. Shepherding was a good life, said Walt, who looks every inch a shepherd, with those clear piercing eyes.

July 22

Lizzie and I rode again in the evening, along the Green Lane above Dog Dean. A gipsy family had just set up their half cylindrical tent. A woman was asleep by the smoky fire, and a small girl of about three, with flaxen hair, and a curiously old face, played with a puppy. A man, swarthy and about 35, obligingly held his pony as we rode by.

July 23

We spent all day at Titchbourne, picking up spuds by the bucketful, and filling up the sacks. Every one wanted to know how I had got on with the thatch drawing, could I thatch a rick now? How many clumps could I draw in an hour? And so on. It was very hot and thundery all day.

July 24

We were all back at the spuds in this morning, going up the humpy bit, where the soil is extra sandy, because of a flourishing bury. The spuds were also scabby from sawfly. It was very hot, with a clear blue sky. A most beautiful view. In the foreground, were 40 young Short-horn heifers, mostly roan. A nice looking bunch. To the left was Hangall Copse, with its dark green oaks and birches, embellished by a solitary splash of yellow ragwort. Straight ahead of us was Brinson's. Like Pete's it is an old brick farmhouse covered with ivy. Strangely enough, the adjacent Dutch barn, with its bright pink corrugated iron roof, did not look in the least bit out of place in the landscape. A little beyond was Bowman's cottage, nestling in the shade of Lowden's Copse, and after that the forested undulations fade into the deep blue distance, with the famous silver fir standing out on the horizon, a full firs height, above the other trees. Bowman paid us a visit in the afternoon. He always does turn up some time or other, with his gun and corduroy jacket, looking every inch a textbook keeper.

July 25

My last day but one. We finished the spuds by 4pm. On my leaving, Walt said aloud: 'I reckon Jane's one of the best'. And Titch seemed sorry about my departure, as were Carter, Lizzie and Paddy. I don't know about the taciturn pair, Fred and Pat.

July 26

I'm sorry to be leaving 'Titch' where it was always fun. I spent all day at Rangers, hoeing mangolds. I said goodbye to the affable Boss and his wife, and they asked me to be sure and look in whenever I could.

July 27

Another hot oppressive day. I biked to Bowerchalke, at the far end of the Ebble or Chalke Valley. As I climbed the steep round face of Marleycombe, it started to spot with rain, and I just made the shelter of the Ox Drove before it got too heavy. It was too hazy to see the Isle of Wight, and Pentridge and Damerham Knoll looked distant. On the Chase between Chicken Grove and Vernditch, walking was very rough. Some of the droves are badly overgrown. This is the countryside where many a bloody battle took place between Keepers and Poachers. At one time the Chase extended almost as far as Salisbury. I walked along the old Roman road that ran between Sorbiodunum and Dorchester. I managed to find the place where Grims Ditch starts up again beside a dried up dewpond. There was threshing going on in dreadful heat. I walked back on to the Ox Drove, finally leaving it to take the track down to Bishopstone. Masses of butterflies about, mostly clouded yellows and marble whites.

July 29

I walked over to Yarnbury. It was sunny and a hot breeze whispered in the fast ripening barley, across which a host of white butterflies drifted and danced against a leaden sky. This time I walked parallel with the main track, and watched the cocksfoot being loaded on to a trailer. Further on by Bushes Farm, bales of hay dotted the big pasture. A large machine that moved along the wakes was churning them out slowly. Bushes is farmed by the War Department. Where the track turns into a wasteland of ragwort, the ground is covered with rough turf, patches of bare chalk, and yet more ragwort! The whole area is littered with empty bomb cases, all of which were tenanted by rabbits, and as I walked past there were constant clanging sounds as the rabbits hastily evacuated! Over by Chitterne Barn, I saw a Sparrow Hawk perched in an elm. Threshing was going on. Once in Chitterne itself, I walked the four miles to Codford, and got a hitch home.

LANDSCAPE
A leaden sky,
Heavy with heat;
Clouds of white butterflies
Drifting and dancing,
Whirling like snowflakes
Carelessly indolent
Whitening the kale.
Resurgent Plain,
Chalk tracks glaring;
White shadowed beech clumps
Stud the horizon.
Out of the sunken way,
Yellow with ragwort,
Leaps a young rabbit.
A kestrel poised
In checked momentum,
Swiftly seeks shelter.
Latently ponderous
Down fall the first big drops,
As round the ripened oats
Moves the slow binder.
J.E.H. 1947

August 1

I hitched to Sixpenny Handley, not an interesting village visually. I walked straight through it, and along the road turning into Cranborne Chase where the woods meet the road. I was thrilled to see considerable quantities of silver washed fritillaries in the open drives, and also a few pearl bordered, silver washed were everywhere, sunning themselves and flitting on to the ever-present ragwort in the glades. There were also a few commas, and speckled woods.

I came down by South Lodge into Tollard Royal where King John once had a hunting lodge. I had planned to take my favourite route back, via Ashcombe Bottom, but it came on to rain heavily, and I was fortunate to hitch a beer lorry going to Ludwell. I sat aloft on a beer barrel, wrapped in the driver's old Mac! I didn't know the road, but even in the rain the views were superb, giving me a new angle on Quarry and Ashcombe Bottoms. How sparsely the grass grows on those chalk heights, and of course ragwort everywhere. I could see over the wooded chase to distant Pentridge in the south. Ahead was Wingreen, short of 1,000 feet, but one of the highest points in Wiltshire, and just short of the Dorset border. Its beech clump takes the full force of the gales.

Once the lorry reached the crest of the down, a wide panoramic view was spread out which included Shaftesbury on its hilltop, Whitesheet Hill, where the old Shaston–Sarum coach road descends to the Vale, Grovely Woods and the Plain, as far as distant Martinsell, another high point above the Pewsey Vale. Immediately below, lie the flat fields of Ferne, the neat-hedged fields on the Dorset border, the Donheads, Bartshill and Wardour Castle.

August 8

In the evening I biked to Wylye, along the main road. Then turned back along the lower lane as far as Little Langford, with its tiny church surrounded by fine chestnut trees. On the down below Grovely, harvesting was in progress, three tractors and trailers busily going to and fro, and two ricks being built. On the edge of the woods barley and wheat were in hile. As I stopped to put up some fallen hiles, a tractor and binder was moving round the remaining barley. It was breezy and sunny. I watched a roe deer grazing, or do they browse? I love Grovely best in the evenings; there is such a blending of sun and deep shadow. It was 8:30pm and the harvesters were just putting up the last load, when I thought I heard Stone Curlews? Up to now I have only seen them on the far side of the wood on Barford Down.

September 10

I took a Wilts and Dorset bus as far as Willoughby Hedge, and struck off for Keysley, along a barely visible track. Keysley is a lovely looking old farmhouse, protected from the wind by somewhat battered beech trees. On the adjacent down were a lot of Longhorn crossed with Hereford cattle. Rather an unusual strain. I spoke to an old labourer thatching a rick. He thought we were in for a mild winter. Let's hope so after last year.

I walked on over the downs as far as Brixton Deverill, and called in on Mr and Mrs Jones at Riversdale, a plain but pleasant house, with a slate roof. The little River Deverill runs through the garden, lower down it becomes the Wylye. Mrs Jones told me that the manor house opposite, across the way, had been a monastery. When the monks were turned out and dispossessed by Henry VIII and the infamous Thomas Cromwell they cursed the place, saying that no one who dwelt there would enjoy happiness. What happened in past years I know not, but according to Mrs Jones, during her time in Brixton, one owner had gone bankrupt, a second fell from a horse and broke his neck, and his son had blown his brains out. A tragic sequence of events, and if she is to be believed, which I have no reason to doubt, the present owners are far from enjoying a state of unalloyed bliss.

Propped against the wall of the church, is an old stone coffin, said to belong to one of King Alfred's men, killed somewhere in the locality in a skirmish with the Danes, prior to the battle of the White Horse at Bratton, not far away as the crow flies! The locals say there will never be peace in the church until it is buried again. I had intended to walk back over Little Down to Tytherington but they were insistent I stay to tea, after which they drove me to Warminster to catch a bus.

September 11

I was woken by the bleating of sheep passing through the village on their way to Wilton Fair. There has been no rain since August 6. Everything is looking brown and shrivelled. Alison and I hitched to Tollard Royal, quite a feat in itself, as there is so little traffic on the Blandford road. We walked up Ashcombe Bottom. There were fewer rabbits than usual and plenty of nuts on the hazels. A pair of Jays screamed raucously ahead of us through the sycamores leading to the farm cottages. We walked boldly through the courtyard of Ashcombe House, which appeared deserted – no sign of the caretaker.

We watched as a pair of Buzzards wheeled and spiralled over Win Green, the sun turning their feathers to bronze. The sky was a brilliant blue, with few white clouds. We lay on our tummies and watched the cloud shadows drift across

Winklebury Camp, with its 40-foot-high ramparts; possibly the furthest point from which one can glimpse, on a clear day, the tip of the Cathedral spire. We came down into Ferne and crossing the flat expanse of stubble, I picked up a perfect fossil of a cockleshell.

September 17

I bussed to Heytesbury and walked through Tytherington and past Haycombe to Parsonage Down, where it was quite strange to see oats uncut and flattened in a year when elsewhere everything has long been gathered in. The gipsies are camped on Rook Hill, which is well named. I have seldom seen so many congregating in one spot! I walked on over Little Down, and ended up again at the Jones' for tea. This time conversation turned to witchcraft. When they were living in a remote Devon village, long before the war, two young men were charged with burning a 'Witch' and were given seven years for manslaughter. To the disgust of the villagers, whose attitude was, 'Well what else could they have done, she being a Witch!' Chucked her in the village pond perhaps? Sounds incredible in such recent times! After tea Reggie (Jones) took me for a walk on Cold Kitchen Down behind the house. It is another high point in S.W. Wiltshire. From it we could pick out all the familiar landmarks. Win Green, the Great Ridge Wood, Clay Hill, Scratchbury Camp, Alfred's Tower, etc. At the base of Cold Kitchen, beautifully set, is a remote farm, Woodcombe. It stands in a combe of the same name, very remote and isolated. It nestles among trees and has a pink tin roof, but it looks and blends in well. The surrounding down is sheepwalk that has been given over to heifers. A shame as the springy turf is no more; it is all bents, with no velvet sheen. A Roman road fords the river at Kingston Deverill, and climbs up over Cold Kitchen. Kitchen in fact denotes the former presence of Romans. Possibly it was the site of an inn? We came back through Bushcombe, which has a large population of foxes and badgers.

September 24

Alison and I biked along the lower lane from Wilton. Under the tall elms just beyond Wishford a weasel shot across the road in front of us. We stopped abruptly and dismounted, and I started to call the weasel, as I was taught by Norris the Water Bailiff. The little creature at once came out from the grass verge, and stood on its hind paws, looking at us quizzically, until Alison's shrieks of delight sent it scampering away!

September 26

I hitched a lift to Steeple Langford, walked across to Hanging Langford and on over the down to Grovely. Inside the woods near Ibsbury, the ruined farmyard was full of Wood Pigeon, and rabbits. I walked all over Langford Castle, looking for pottery and coins in the rabbit scratching. The west end of the wood is unknown to me because of the long wartime occupation by the Yanks. Now I decided was the time to explore its interior. It was quite confusing, since there were many parallel tracks, and I only cut across them when necessary, since I noticed signs of R.A.F. traffic. There were empty Nissen huts, and great mounds of ammunition and bombs? A sorry sight in a once peaceful wood.

September 28

Lizzie and I rode the ponies over to Titchhourne on a rather muggy drizzly day. We took the green lane across to Woodstock, crossed Longford Park, and Standlynch Down, where the spindle bushes were a riot of crimsoning leaves and bursting pink berries from which golden seeds were spilling and upon which the Starlings were feeding. We had a grand gallop over Barford Down, and on to Studland where the 'Old woman of the wood' came to her door to wave to us.

October 8

On Upper Farm Down, on the south side of Grovely, I was chatting to Hillier's Shepherd. 'What a good thing,' he said, 'that Jerry did not drop a bomb on Grovely, or half of Wilts would have gone up!' He was most surprised to learn of my excursion through the wood last week, and that I had got safely through, with out being picked up by the R.A.F. It seems they do not allow anyone into that end of the wood without a pass!

October 20

Diana Dunne and I walked through Britford Meadows; we flushed some Teal, about ten in all. We were chatting to Paulson who farms opposite Petersfinger, the Avon being the boundary between the farms. He had a most beautiful collie dog with him. He showed us his gold and silver pheasants in their wire runs. The delicate tracery on their backs and wings would have graced the walls of an Islamic Mosque.

November 1

The Municipal Election in Bemerton ward was a contest between Major the Hon Anthony Herbert – Cons and Mrs Eastman – Labour (re-standing). From 10:00am

– noon, I telled at the school (Bemerton) and Mr Maple telled for Labour. Mrs Eastman flounced in and I said 'Good morning' but was completely ignored by her, not even a nod, as a piece of Tory dirt!

In the afternoon it was very wet but I wandered off into the water meadows for an hour or so then returning, on impulse, I went straight to the parish rooms where I found Mr and Mrs Love counting for Tony Herbert and Mr and Mrs Harding counting for Mrs Eastman, both seeing who had voted, etc, and who hadn't. At that point the Herbert clan rolled up with a luxurious fleet of cars. Lady P. at her most affable! Tony Herbert, raffish-looking, hair on end, yellow waistcoat, resembling 'Dizzy' without the kiss curls. The Hon David never grows any older. Mary Herbert was there and Richard Pennoyer, Lady P's nephew. And there was me, with dripping wet hair, wearing a once posh windcheater of Alison's with a large rent in one arm! At this point Mr Love gave me sheets of names to round up and I was sent off with Richard Pennoyer. We toured around Bemerton in his beautiful American Packard, picking up elderly voters and canvassing madly – all great fun. Richard, known as Kim, had a quiet manner, was easy to talk to and restful to be with. He works in London for Ranks and comes to his Mother's cottage at Stapleford for weekends. So of course we talked of Yarnbury and Stapleford Castles and he told me to try and get a copy of *Ladies Whose Bright Eyes* [by Ford Madox Ford] It's about Stapleford Castle in the middle ages. I will try at Beach's tomorrow.

Apparently, his aunt, Lady P., said good morning to Mrs Eastman when she met her at the polls and the silly woman just stuck her head in the air and walked off! Lady P. roared with laughter, the best thing she could have done. Soon we were rushing round in the dark. We rounded up quite a lot who weren't going to vote. Later in the evening I biked into Salisbury to hear the results at the Guildhall. They weren't out until 9:45. I managed to get right to the front. Herbert got in! We never thought he would, with a majority of 39! I cheered and clapped, while two Labour ladies near me booed. Mrs Eastman then came to the mike and one of the two ladies presented her with a bouquet of red and white carnations. She made a dreadful speech but well-spoken and retired smirking!

Councillor Hall got in for Milford and there were shouts of 'good old Sid and good old Dixie' as two other stalwarts were returned. Also Hancock with his beard and draping black garments.

November 3

I went into the Morrison Hall with a list for Tommy Tucker (Conservative agent for John Morrison MP). Tucker said, 'I was hoping to see you. You know you won the election for us!' So I felt very pleased and several other people came up and congratulated me. I also heard that Mrs Eastman was taking her defeat very badly, raving and muttering. And Major Herbert told the working men's club in Bemerton that Mrs E had refused to shake hands with him after the results.

November 10

I went to Mayor Making. I think Gordon should be a good one. He speaks well and he is not lost for words, nor does he lack the ability to utter them, which has been the distinctive failing of several of our Mayors in the last three years. I am going to attend council meetings when ever possible, as I am horrified to find how little I know of local government. It was quite an impressive ceremony. Our civic fathers looked very dignified, especially Hancock and Rambridge. The Mayor spoke, saying that prior to 1939, 50% control was in the hands of the city; today all but 24% is managed by Whitehall. Yet local government contributed much to England's former prosperity and Whitehall government is out of touch and unimaginative. It is wrong that the prerogatives of citizens should be wrested from them. I believe that had this occurred a century ago there would have been insurrection all over the country. We take the loss of our liberties too placidly.

November 15

In the afternoon, I walked up to Yarnbury from Steeple Langford. It was cold but sunny, with a nip of frost in the air that made my cheeks glow. In stark contrast to the bare grey-brown of the downs, Yarnbury showed up in dark green relief. The totally bare, rather uninteresting stretch of down that surrounds Cliffe Bottom, formed a perfect complete picture, because of the banking clouds above it. The clouds and their shadows made it. Without them, as scenery it was nothing. They showed us the beauty of the curve, and softened the outline, making it pleasing to the eye. That particular piece of down is unrelieved by so much as a juniper or thorn.

Emerging from what I call 'The Valley of the Shadow', where Yarnbury disappears momentarily from sight only to re-emerge on this occasion with long black, streaky clouds running across it (spectacular, against a blue sky), I ran up over the ramparts, and there in the centre, were a mingled group of sheep and cattle. On Cow Down, the Lapwings were wheeling and crying mournfully, one moment black, and the next silver. On Cowdown and Yarnbury troubles become insignificant. There is such a feeling of Eternal Agelessness, quite inexpressible! When I left by Cliffe Bottom, the sun was setting in a burst of golden glory over Bilbury Rings, at the western extremity of Grovely.

INTANGIBILITY

In Grovely, the charcoal-burner's smoke
Hangs blue above the bracken's dying fire;
The Jays have striped the acorns from the oak
And in my heart has kindled wild desire.
By sudden gusts the sodden leaves are torn
And red the berries on the lichened thorn.
Bleached is the grass along the age old way,
But still the rain blacked heads of knapweed tell
The purple pageantry of yesterday:
Now lost, yet still unbroken in its spell,
Only the sun in dying splendour flings
A shaft of light enkindling Bilbury Rings.
From Cow Down where the plovers wheel, and cry
In mournful ecstasy, I turn to where
Green ramparts fretted, dark against a sky
Of lucient loveliness and radiance rare.
Entranced I watched each lingering line of light
Flicker and fade, fast ebbing into night.
From Yarnbury's walls I watch the darkness fold
Lynchett and barrow till it fills the Plain
With ancient wraiths and stories still untold,
Bringing forgotten memories back again.
The wind and I our lonely vigil keep
And share the solitude with Night and sheep.
J.E.H. 1947

November 20

I walked from Manor Farm Chilmark to Wylye. It gets dark so early now I can't go far. It was a filthy sort of day, with a persistent thin mizzle of rain, and poor visibility. I followed the line of the ditch to the deserted farmhouse on Wylye Down, where it stands and crumbles in the shelter of a beech grove. The farm buildings are still in use. They stand on the edge of a deep, bare combe, on the sides of which are some of the best and most distinctive Celtic fields I know. I came back by Bilberry Rings, and I had to walk to South Newton in the dark and rain, having managed to lose half my bus fare!

November 25

I needed to go to Tilshead to pay Mrs Kyte for eggs. I bussed to Stapleford and walked from there. It was very hard going on Cow Down, as far as Yarnbury. A strong gale made it almost impossible to stand upright. It was a case of two steps forward and one back! The Plain was a picture pattern of pale green wheat, the bleached brownish white of dead grass; over on Berwick Down a dark green splodge of kale, and beside it, dark brown plough. The sky and the Plain were made to compliment each other! Although the wind was so strong and cold, the sky was blue with little fluffy grey and white clouds. By Yarnbury, ploughing was going on. Near Fox Covert, there were so many rabbits that I gave chase, but they quickly disappeared down the myriad holes! I walked on by Cope Hill, and White Barrow with its ancient box cover, where the Wood Pigeons love to nest in spring. On the way home the wind abated, and in the vicinity of Fox Covert, a small charm of Goldfinches were dipping up and down among the clumps of withered nodding thistles. A few spread out Larks, rose and fell, in front of me as I walked.

Instead of returning by Yarnbury, I came out on to the road, near Winterbourne Stoke, and immediately got a lift to Berwick St James. From there I climbed the track called the Langford Way. Suddenly, from a large expanse of stubble a large grey bird rose up in front of me. I was surprised to see a Heron! A few yards further on, six more rose up in front of me, and flapped away towards the valley, legs trailing. I could hardly believe my eyes! I wonder what they were after on that exposed piece of ground? I mentioned this to Canon Borlase in the evening and he told me that a man at Bishopstone, had recently shot 25!

November 26

Today's hitch took me to Hindon, where I admired the holly tree in the churchyard, which bore a heavy crop of berries. So far the only tree I have seen this year well and truly laden! The day was sunny, windy and frosty, with a blue sky. I went by Hawking Down and Pertwood bushes, to Pertwood to look at the little Norman church, alone on the down, in a surround of nettles and beech trees. From there I could see over to Cold Kitchen and the Knolls. The latter resemble the long necks of headless horses, with beech trees forming the manes.

Smoke was rising from the bushy lane that leads past Rook Hill. From the smell, not unpleasant, I knew it was Gipsy smoke. Sure enough on rounding a corner I saw the caravan and the children. A little further on, when descending the western end of the Ridge Wood, smoke drifted across the greensward in front of me. I paused, instinctively, and there just inside the wood, behind a screen of bare hazels, and oaks, I saw a young man, in an air force flying jacket, fanning the flames of a fire with a handkerchief. I slipped noiselessly past, down into Well Bottom, as quickly as possible. Instinct told me something was not quite right. The man did not belong there. He wasn't a woodman. The bottom was filled with a large herd of polled Aberdeens. I climbed the steep slope, ran down the far side, and up again on to Corton Down, finally coming out at Upton Lovell.

November 27

Mrs Drury, (wife of the Rector of Wilton), kindly lent me her Rolleiflex, so that I might photograph the Gipsies, if I could find them again. It was a very poor day for photography, misty frosty, with flat pasty clouds, and a grey sky. As I expected the Gipsies had left Rook Hill. Their camping site displayed the usual signs of their passage. Old socks, the odd shoe, and bits of jersey, a new clothes peg and chrysanthemum, whittled from hazel and dyed orange. A farm boy I ran into told me that they had not been gone long, which I had deduced from the fresh pony droppings. I followed the trail on to the down. The weather became very cold and even more overcast, though the distant plain towards Imber was picked out by streaks of sunlight from a surround of grey haze. The track forked to the right, and there in the hedgerow, above the Tytherington Lane, were two caravans and some children sitting round a fire. One was an intelligent looking boy of about twelve nursing a whippet pup. The others ranged in age from about seven to a year old. The usual 'dirty tousled brats'! A middle-aged woman appeared from inside a van, and picked up the youngest child. After saying 'good day', I asked if I might take their photograph? 'No, gipsies do not like to be photographed.' She was most insistent in her refusal, saying that a lady from Sutton Veny had wanted to do so, but she had refused to allow it! 'Is it supposed to be unlucky?' I asked. (Wondering if she was afraid of the evil eye?) 'No, but Gipsies don't like to be seen!' I changed the subject and we talked about the difficulties caused by rationing. After which I said, 'Look! If you will let me take photos, I will send you copies.'

The bargain was happily accepted, and she said, 'Would I just wait for the ponies? I must take a picture of the baby on a pony!' In a short while, two hairy, filthy, villainous looking men appeared, leading the ponies. The gipsy lady ordered one of them to be bought hither. The baby was placed on its back, and promptly began to howl! The other children clustered round. I took two pictures, and one of the eldest lads, back view beside a caravan. The two men, whose looks belied them, were very polite. I greased the lady's palm with half a crown, and offered to bring the photos over for them, but it appeared that they were off to Somerset. I am to

send them to Freda Barney, c/o the Post Office, Warminster, to await arrival! For a
joke I asked the eldest girl if she told fortunes. 'Oh yes.' She seized my hand, saying
I was to have a stroke of luck before Christmas, and a holiday at the seaside! Pathetic!

As I walked on down the lane a Sparrow Hawk dashed out in front of me,
with a Blackbird in its talons. Crossing the water meadows at Knook, I watched a
Dipper bobbing about at the water's edge. When I returned her camera, Mrs Drury
said she did not know how I had the nerve to walk in such a lonely places! There's
no nerve required. Funnily enough, yesterday was the only time I felt a slight
unease, and that was because the man did not fit in.

December 5

I walked over to Larkhill with a letter from my father to one of the officers. I went
down the Woodford Valley, and as I approached the farm at Great Durnsford, the air
was alive with a great murmuring coming from the surrounding beech grove.
Naturally I thought it was coming from Starlings, and was surprised to find it came
from a huge concourse of Chaffinches. It was a very dull day, with a sort of mist that
is a kind of thickening of the atmosphere clinging to the folds of the downs.

December 12

Another dull day. I walked from Bathampton to Shrewton, via Yarnbury. Numerous
flocks of Chaffinches, Linnets, and Pigeons. Cutting across Berwick and Parsonage
Down, the vast empty greyness was poignantly lonely, although the down was
dotted with black Aberdeen Angus and Belted Galloways. In the little beech covers,
now bare, the copper leaves rustled under foot but apart from Chaffinches, bird
life was nil.

December 18

Christmas draws near! I biked to Tisbury to look for holly in Haredene Woods,
where hazels were being coppiced. I found a large tree laden with berries,
overhanging an old stone barn! Inside a very old man sat on a stool, plucking
cockerels. Four already plucked, hung from a nail over the lintel. I came home by
Fovant. Sad that since the outbreak of war, the Quidhampton Mummers no longer
come. I loved little Johnnie Jack with his pack upon his back, Father Christmas, the
Turkish Knight, and the Doctor.

December 22

I couldn't sleep, so at 1am I pulled slacks over my pyjamas, put on a jacket, and

– 70 –

went into the water meadows, across the three bridges. It was a still night, and the half moon was brilliantly ornate, hanging low on the horizon. I have never seen anything like the beauty of the stars. There were not many of them, but those that there were, were big and clear as diamonds, and they shone with the translucency of raindrops. The biggest and brightest was Sirius, shining away to the East, below Orion's Belt, and to the West was the reddish glow of Alderbaran.

December 26

BOXING DAY. Heavy rain in the night had left the sky rain-washed blue. It was quite windy. I left my bike at Stapleford Old Castle, and as I crossed the old trackway, and walked parallel with the field of winter wheat, four huge birds flew up from it. For a moment I thought they were Shags! Then I realized they were Geese. They flew off honking across the Wylye towards Grovely Earthworks. They looked like Brents. It was very clear, and the beech clumps on the down stood out distinctly. I walked past Yarnbury and over to Shrewton by the old track to Maddington, then came back by the ruined farm buildings. Heavy black rain clouds hung ominously over the Ridge Wood as I turned for home. Had they swung towards me there was nowhere to shelter in such an empty landscape. Luckily for me it passed on over Heath Hill and Wilton.

December 30

Slight breeze and frosty. Leaving my bike at Upper Woodford, I went on to the downs to photograph Rox Hill Clump, and Westfield. The former at a distance resembles a sailing ship! I walked among the barrows in the Normanton group. There is something eerie about these big barrows, the way they loom between the beech trees covered with the red gold of the fallen leaves. On the open plain I am always conscious of a long forgotten people, but there the barrows do not assert themselves in the same way as they do here among the trees. Almost as if the spirits of the dead were shut in and unable to get away.

I walked on towards Dimonts, a little fir wood, which I have always liked. Col. Baileys' men were bailing straw on Normanton Down. In the bottom I took a picture of the young Under-Shepherd, and Floss, his dog. They were strolling along in front of the sheep. I heard the sheep bells, but a slight undulation of the ground caused me to see the Shepherd and dog before the flock appeared. I think the young man was rather proud to be photographed with the flock (he looked no more than 17). I am sending him a copy. In Spring Bottom, a White Owl flew out from the ghostly larches. In Lake I hitched a lift from Mr Tanner, who is Col.

Bailey's Bailiff. He lives in a super Winchester Caravan, in a clearing just above Lake. On the way home, another White Owl was cruising around the base of Camp Hill, while a Kestrel hung suspended over it.

December 31

I walked up Cliffe Bottom, and over Cow Down. A keen wind was blowing and the sky behind the little fir wood was black. When I came down again, the sun had set, and the sky over Grovely Castle was rich mulberry, streaked with lemon yellow, fading imperceptibly into green.

RETROSPECT

The swiftly passing pageant of the year
Moves on, but I have grasped from its career
Bright images to cheer the winter's gloom
And weave rich tapestries on memory's loom.
The rhapsodising fervour of the lark
From earliest morning until after dark.
The scent of charlock, cowslips on Hoopside
That skirts the ploughland with yellow tide.
There fox cubs tumbled down the earthy banks
Under the twisted thorns, whose lichened flanks
Burgeoned and sagged beneath the weight of may;
Whilst grasses bolted, flowered, till mown for hay.
On the bare down where rabbits scarred the earth
Pitting with pocks of chalk the thyme starred turf
Where only elder throve, whose chaliced lace
Flaunted its fragrance, drowsed the night's embrace,
With spicy sweetness, filled the summer air.
On wings as silent as the touch of fear
And rounded smooth, the phantom of the field
Spun in and out to seek the evening's yield
Field mouse and vole along the Ivers verge
Through briars and bents where down and ploughland merge;
And campions run a riot of red, to hide
The littered leaflings where the bluebells died.

Here where the trees begin to climb the down
White orchids fashioned for a bridal crown,
Pale ghosts of butterflies impinge the gloom,
And lure the moth with subtle sweet perfume.
Through the long days of drought and torrid heat,
High in the elms that throng the yellowing wheat,
The turtles croon caressing monotones
Or flutter down among the flinty stones
To dust their wings and flirt white bandied tails
While overhead a mewling buzzard sails.
Soon autumn treading hard on summers heels
On misty mornings through the meadow steals
And evening brings pale scattered stars to greet
The screaming swifts that skim the village street.
High on Rook hill, the vagrant gipsies pass
And leave behind these tokens on the grass,
A pony's droppings and an ancient sock
The tattered remnants of a baby's frock,
A clothes peg, and a gay chrysanthemum,
Whittled from hazel by a skilful thumb.
Now as the old year sinks to its decline,
It is as if the tired sap turned to wine
And all the hedgerow trees in copse and spinneys
Are gaily gowned, the elms spill golden guineas.
The beech stands deep in copper that will lie
Till buds unfold once more against the sky
Their delicate green tissue to the sun
When springs eternal saga is begun.
J.E.H. 1947

Cold Kitchen from Woodcombe, 17 September 1947

Gipsies on Tytherington Down, 27 November 1947

Corton Down Barn, 26 November 1947

Under-shepherd on Normanton Down, 30 December 1947

Sheepfold, Smithen Down, 12 February 1950

Hobby at nest with young, 7 August 1950

Ibsbury from Horsemead, 1950

Yellow Wagtail's nest, Spring 1950

Little Owl at nest, 5 June 1950

1st and 2nd Fields, River Nadder, 30 July 1950

A kitten bounded over stepping-stones, 26 June 1950

A corner of Compton Chamberlayne

Stapleford and River Till

Sun and shadow, Knook Down

Jane and Paddy at Titchbourne, 1947

1948

January 4

I hitched to Fisherton de la Mere, and walked through the little laurel wood to Parry's Barn (now Jeans' Barn). At the start it was windy and cold, with the sun trying in fits and starts to break through. I talked to a nice old man who was cutting kale. In spite of the heavy rain in the night, the wind had dried it out. I kept to the right of Box Cover, where men were busy pulling up the Box. Once in the Bottom there was nothing to be seen but bare down and sky. Until suddenly, with a loud quacking, five Mallards rose up from the dewpond. I looked back to drink in the intoxicating beauty of the Plain. Towards Tilshead, the sky was pale blue, merging into deep blue overhead, with a few streaky clouds over the distant plain. On looking back over the Ridge Wood, and Grovely, the sunlight flooded the way I had come and accentuated the small bosky coverts, while at the same time, softening the folds of down. Over Chitterne Barn, the sunlight and shade lay in moving patches and the wind carried the sound of the sheep bells from Hooper's lambing pens. The newly ploughed piece of Cow Down that runs alongside the track was being diced and harrowed by two tractors. After lunch I did a quick flip on my bike to Wilton, and on through Bulbridge to the top of Bishopstone Hill, in order to get a last fill of Wiltshire air. Tomorrow I am off to London for three months. At the top of the Hare Warren I glanced at my watch – 2pm exactly. I let myself go full tilt down the hill, and with the wind at my back, reached the Square in two minutes flat!

The reason for my going to London was, that my Aunt had foreseen (and it did not take much foresight!) that servants would be in short supply, and that it would be a wise thing for me to acquire housewifery, and some of the culinary skills. A cousin had recently completed two courses running concurrently, one in the daytime at the London Poly taught the rudiments of dress making, household know how, and how to cook, making the best of small rations. All very sensible! The students worked in pairs, and cooked and ate their own lunch each day. In contrast, the other course was Constance Spry. Older women attended it, now staffless! They arrived in fur coats and diamond brooches, and appeared to have limitless access to eggs, butter and cream. Needless to say I booked in for the Poly, and stayed in a cosy South Ken hotel. From August the same year, I had booked in as a student at Lower Langford in North Somerset . . . but that lay ahead.

February 15

Dying for country air, I took the train to Salisbury and from there a bus to Steeple Langford. It way a perfect sunny day, the air soft and balmy, almost spring like. Along the banks of the Wylye, the alder catkins shone gold. On the curved slopes of Cow Down, the sheep were grazing. Instead of walking through the 'Valley of the Shadow', I climbed up to the beech clump, and from there, on looking over to the little fir wood, I could see the lambing pens. The air was filled to overflowing with their clamorous bleating. Most ewes had twins, some only a few hours old. They butted their tiny heads into the sides of the ewes, and tugged at their teats frenziedly, tails wagging. Over Yarnbury, the larks were singing, and the Partridges were paired. It won't be long now before the Wheatear returns. In the field by Stapleford Castle, one of the two white-faced mares had foaled. It was donkey coloured, a dusty grey-brown that faded into white on the legs. The cottage gardens, all nicely sheltered, were filled with snowdrops, aconites, primulas, and pink bell-like flowers of elephant's ear. In sheltered corners, on the lower branches, the hawthorns were in leaf.

March 8

It's wondrous to be home! Alison and I went to the Larkhill Point-to-Point to celebrate. It was a sunny day with an east wind – 'Blackthorn Winter'! I won four of the races, on which I betted. Alison one. We both had our money on Doughcake, a very safe bet and a popular win!

March 30

Rain and wind, but nothing daunted. I walked in ' Para'. In Arcadia was a Keeper's Gibbet, enough to make you weep. Hung on it were eight Magpies, five Little Owls, two Jays, one Kestrel, two Hedgehogs, three Stoats and two Weasels. All freshly killed, and all because of an aristocrat's desire to rear Pheasants! To my mind the Little Owl and Kestrel should not have been there, and I would never grudge a Hedgehog a few eggs.

April 1

I heard the Cuckoo at 4:00a.m.! It has been a warm sunny day. The cowslips were out on Cowdown and the Larks were singing. One perched on a tussock near me, and sung its heart out.

April 2

Squally, sunny with a rain-washed sky. I met Henry in Hindon and we walked back to Brixton Deverill and had lunch at 'Riversdale'. Afterwards we walked up Cold Kitchen in a very stiff wind. Coming round Brimsdown it suddenly began to hail with such force and profusion as I have never experienced before. The hailstones were the size of large peas. It was most unpleasant on our faces, but exhilarating too. We made the edge of the wood and watched it sheeting down into Bidcombe Bottom, blotting out the trees and sides of the coomb. It was a dramatic spectacle lasting just a few brief minutes. It stopped, the sun came out, the down was white with patches of mauve where the violets grew. Henry, very nice, easy to talk to – what eyelashes! I was quite envious.

April 3

The Rawlence's gave a party to celebrate Mary's wedding in the USA. Great to re-meet many old friends, but a hint of sadness remembering those who were not present. All lost in the War. Dear Edward, Mary's brother, killed on the Leopold Canal in Belgium. Gerald Miles, who went down on the destroyer Penelope at Nettuno. Ronnie Martin, last seen by me marching past St John's church with a lot of other lads under the command of a sergeant. It was the first day of the War and we were just coming out of church. He was in the Fleet Air Arm, and drowned at sea saving another rather than himself.

April 18

Walked around Horse Mead, blackthorn still blooming, kingcups glorious. Saw the White Owl fly out of a willow and a young man playing with his golden retriever. Delightful scene full of joie de vivre. Caught a bus back and surprise! Henry was on it. We're going to walk again next Sunday and he is coming to tea. In the evening Alison and I biked to Britford.

TO AN UNKNOWN YOUNG MAN
The Years have claimed and swept away
That tranquil sun-washed April day.
When water meadows spring-patrolled
Were carpeted with king cup gold
Leaping with ease the sluggish stream
A golden dog and golden boy

Ran laughing for ecstatic joy
While I who watched them share the glee of that Elysian rhapsody.
Now unrelenting wet was May
Tall willows wept in shrouds of grey
And battered hawthorns cast around
Their rain seared blossoms to the ground
Despondent boy on river seat,
Despondent dog bowed at his feet,
And nameless cares upon your brow
Without a sign of laughter now!
While I who passed you sighed to see
How fleeting is all ecstasy!
J.E.H. 1948

April 21

The chestnuts, oaks and elms are full leaf. The woods are full of bluebells, and in the water meadows, the new green of the willows is dusted over with yellow catkins and their pollen. A Plover zoomed up from a clump of reeds, and ran off trailing a wing, – the nest was close by. The damp evening air exuded the scents of growing grass, warm cows' breath, and bruised peppermint trampled by their feet.

At the Rectory, the Bartlett's (new Rector and wife) have cut down the old red chestnut stump. It had one live branch growing from the base. It was beautiful and graceful. I had asked them to wait and see it in bloom before doing so. In the evening next day Alison and I walked on Lake Down, and found a Pheasant's nest with 12 brown eggs, under a box bush, and watched a heifer chase a hare down a slope.

April 23

We wandered about at the Great Ridge. Half way up the right-hand track to the woods from Codford, we ate our sandwiches sitting under a whitebeam, in which a Blackcap and Willow Wren competed in song. Just inside the wood the Nightingales were singing.

April 26

I took little Gerald out nesting after lunch. I showed him a Linnet sitting on eggs in a hawthorn and a Chaffinch with a beautifully camouflaged nest in a stem of white poplar. She had four eggs. There was a nest of young Song Thrushes, almost fledged, mouth agape and breasts speckled to perfection. In Gipsy Lane, was a Hedge Sparrow sitting on four blue eggs. The nest was at waist height in the hedge, entwined with hop bines. In the same overgrown lane, was another Song Thrush with eggs, and the incomplete nest, which I think is a Whitethroat. A nest of baby Blackbirds had flown. On our way home through the 'first field' we were lucky to find a Mallard's nest, with nine olive green eggs, the downy nest was in the fork of a pollard willow. Later in the evening, biking along the Wishford Lane, a Tawny Owl flew into an elm with a rat in his claws.

April 30

I looked at the Hedge Sparrow's eggs in Gipsy Lane, and they were just hatching. One-minute scrap of ugliness was just out. A cock Cuckoo flew up the lane in front of me, as close as I have ever been to one. He was a lovely slatey blue, with barred breast.

May 5

The hottest day yet! I wore a cotton frock, anxious to cast every clout I could! I left my bike at Savages, and went along Fussel's Lane, where I spotted a Pheasant sitting unusually tightly! I went into Hound Wood, and while I ate lunch, I watched a Willow Wren, a few feet away on a sallow. Blackcaps and Garden Warblers were singing. I came back through Clarendon Woods, and as I emerged on to the down above Savages, there was an old thorn tree, over burdened with may, not a leaf visible. As I pulled down a branch to smell, out flew a Chaffy I had disturbed on her nest.

Biking home by Rangers, I spotted the Hepple boy, who is now a student at 'Pete's', pulling a small harrow behind him up the slope! Something Lizzie and I were spared! In the evening, which was a perfect golden one, I walked about the meadows beyond Wishford. The bushes were smothered with may, and the water crowfoot was out on the stream. Fish were rising every few seconds. I sat on Horsemead Hatch and talked to the cowman's boys, who were out nesting. They took me to see a Magpie's nest in an old thorn, and a Moorhen's, which had been built high up in an alder. A White Owl flew past us.

May 8

A glorious sunny day! I took sandwiches and went back to Wishford, and strolled about the meadow in the Serrington direction. A Kingfisher winged its way up stream, and a pair of Dabchicks appeared and disappeared. 'Now you see me, now you don't'! Their heads bobbed up like periscopes. Feeling lazy, I sat on Horsemead Hatch, idly flipping through the pages of Richard Jefferies's *Story of my Heart*, when there was a rustle in the bushes, and sounds of panting. Next moment a large golden retriever, tongue out, tail wagging, was standing beside me. A slim young man closely followed her with hair like thistledown. I stood up to let them pass, and we stood for a moment, each trying to recollect where we had seen each other before. I said, 'Haven't we met before?' 'Yes,' he said, 'I've been trying to think where, since I saw you by the river last Sunday'. 'Municipal Elections?' 'Yes, of course!' He had driven me in his Packard all around Bemerton Ward last November, bringing aged and infirm voters to the polls, and trying to persuade those still undecided to vote for his cousin, Tony Herbert! After that we talked a bit, chiefly about the state of the world. He was undecided as to whether to leave the country or not. I said, 'Wouldn't it be a bit like leaving a sinking ship?' and he agreed. On the other hand, he was half American and his father was out there at the moment: something to do with the Marshall Plan. He had fought in Italy during the War. We had a bit of a laugh about Sir Stafford Cripps' new car, which for propaganda purposes had been put over as a Ford, but which was in fact a Rolls Royce! He lives in London and works for J.Arthur Rank. His mother has a cottage where the Till and Wylye meet, so he comes down most weekends. I've been told I can fish there whenever I want. An amusing incident recounted by Kim took place while his aunt was canvassing at the last general election. One old lady announced that she was going to vote 'communist' because she regularly attended Holy Communion!

May 11

A nest I found half finished in Gipsy Lane, some time ago is a Blackcap's with four eggs in it. Also in the lane is a nest with half-fledged Hedge Sparrows. They're covered with black down and at the ugly stage. Two Chaffies nests, the young nearly fully fledged and one 'ragged' nest, as the village boys call it.

I came home at teatime to hear that Edith Olivier had died [author, literary patron and first woman mayor of Wilton]. A great loss to the county. My particular memory of a visit to the Daye House, is of Edith reclining elegantly on her chaise longue, smoking an Egyptian cigarette in her long yellow holder as we talked about interesting visitors to Wilton House, including my adolescent hero – Sir Philip Sidney.

Edith was the first person to call on Granny and the aunts when they left Ireland for Bemerton in 1916.

May 15

I decided to take up the invitation to fish at Tilsend. So I set off for Stapleford with my fishing gear. I walked round to the front of the cottage and saw an old gardener cum retainer, and as no one else appeared to be about except Judy the dog, I explained to him why I had come. 'You'll be wanting Master Kim,' he said and at that moment 'Master Kim' leant out of an upstairs window and said, 'Good morning, have you come to fish? Go right down, the pool on the left is the best.' I went ahead. What I took to be a backwater of the Wylye is actually the end of the Till. I caught two trout, threw one back and lost a big one. At 3:30 Kim went off across the meadows with Judy. He came back and sat on the bank opposite and talked. He seemed rather upset that his mother was going off to America, so I asked if he would be coming down as usual. He said he thought so. Then he is going off to Italy in August with an art professor. He was fighting in Italy during the War. He had just seen Laurence Olivier in Hamlet, as had I, so we discussed that and other films. He often goes up to Grovely, he said, and watches the deer. He can't understand how anyone can shoot them because they are too pretty. He said he had worked with the German prisoners when they were digging out the Wylye, and that they worked like machines and never seemed to tire! Then he said, 'Goodbye, come again, just walk in!' Then I said goodbye to his mother and offered her the fish, which she said to keep as they had plenty. Funnily enough, with her was Lady Pembroke's eccentric cousin 'Billy' from Pembroke canteen days.

May 18

I walked up to Ibsbury in the evening and climbed into the big beech on the edge of the wood. It was glorious with the wind soughing in the branches, and rustling the leaves and on the grass beneath the hares were quietly feeding.

May 20

I biked up the Wylye Valley to Bapton, and then climbed on to Stockton Down. I saw a Stone Curlew in Starveall Bottom. The sun shone, the sky was blue and the breeze warm. I lay among the milkwort and watched the mounted shepherd rounding up the sheep on the slope opposite. The larks were singing and hens' feathers were littered about outside the fox's earth. To my astonishment, hidden among the bushes, and just inside the wood itself, were tanks, and army lorries, and ack-ack guns all covered over with camouflage nettings, and all made of rubber? Whatever it was, they were fake!

Alone, on a bare stretch of ground, stands the umbrella tree, the only shelter for sheep and they usually cluster around it. The wind-swept position has caused the branches to grow up thickly from the trunk like tangled hair. Down in the bottom near Strattons, were a crowd of marsh frits: they feed on devils' bit scabious, and the caterpillars spin a web on it, in which they spent the winter. Alas, a Blackcap's nest in Gipsy Lane on which I had been keeping an eye has been ragged!

May 27

I hitched to Ansty Hollow and climbed over the down and up on to the Old Coach Road. There is a ruined cottage in the little beech wood at the top, where white hellebores grow. This year there are fewer than usual. The gipsies were camped in a slight hollow just off the road. There were three terriers on guard, beside five smartly painted vans. Looking across the steeply wooded sides of Norrington Combe, I saw a sandy fox lollop up the side where trees have been felled and over to the copse beyond. The dewpond near the road on Middle Down is one of the best preserved I know, so many of them are dried up and a sunken hollow is all that is left. In the evening I fished at Tilsend. Some Moorhens had just hatched and the sooty chicks were being brooded by their mother.

May 31

After supper I biked to the Hare Warren, and on along the coach road. Grovely opposite lay bathed in sunlight, but Teffont Woods and the Chilmark Ridge, were blurred by a yellow haze. On the other side the Ox Drove was very clear. The way ahead of me was alive with rabbits, milling in every direction. As I came along the straight with Chislebury ahead, the sun dazzled, bright and glaring before sinking below the ramparts. I walked about on Knapp Down, where a boy was popping at rabbits and turned off down to Fifield Bavant, passed its little Norman church, one of the smallest in the country. A white owl was hunting in the twilight around Broadchalke meadows, and I saw another at Stratford Tony and three Little Owls on the steep hill up to the Race Plain.

June 1

Heavy showers, with bright intervals. I walked through Grovely to Ibsbury. There were great dollops of cuckoo spit on the sallows, and white poplar saplings. I watched two weasels playing.

June 5

Up to Ibsbury again. Sunny and good visibility. On the dewpond by Grovely barn, were two beautiful dragonflies. They were not stream lined and tapering, but thickset and blunted. They chased each other across the surface with such rapidity; it was hard to focus on them. Their bodies were an amethyst blue, the heads black and their wings pale mauve. Families of Great Tits and Marsh Tits with glossy Black Caps were flitting about in the elder and thorn clumps below the fir plantation, near which the wild strawberries were ripening. Along the track to Ibsbury, wild roses and elder were in bloom.

June 11

It has been rather a heavy thundery day with sunny periods. In the clearings in Clarendon Woods, viper's bugloss was flowering; some of the clumps were over two foot tall! I love the tight pink buds that uncurl, fern-like, into blue flowers. Some of them were covered with cinnabar moths, all scarlet and black. There were spires of dyers rocket, some as much as four foot tall, also pyramidal orchids, twayblades, and tall thistles turning purple, as summer nears its zenith. Grey squirrels abounded. In the evening I went again to Ibsbury; a heat haze obscured the view. A hare walked past without seeing or smelling me.

June 17

A dull day with heavy showers, but I was set on going to Berwick St James, so off I went the long way by Druids Lodge. I wanted to see if the water lilies were out on the dewpond, just beyond the cattle shelter. There were, and quite the finest I have seen. Such immaculate perfection and in such an unexpected site. Who could have put them there? Afterwards at Ibsbury, growing in the rough grass, which was sopping wet, were fragrant, marsh, and pyramidal orchids. In the woods near the old barn, I met a young fox. It kept walking and stopping, as if uncertain of its whereabouts, and taking no notice of the baby rabbit only feet away from it. It was loosing its baby coat, and rather streaky looking. I came down to Kingsmead, where the Swifts were skimming low over the river. The flies in the Wishford Lane were as bad as ever. Between Wishford and Golden's they were swarming so madly that I had to close my eyes and bike blind.

June 24 (St John's Eve)

Warm, with bright intervals, very muggy. I walked all over Berwick Down, from the Langford Way to Yarnbury, including all the down above Berwick. It's one of my favourite parts of the Plain, and once off the tracks, as lonely as any of it. It is a basin of bare down, and lynchets. Scattered beech clumps lend it character. Wheatears were chattering in great numbers, chiefly around the rabbit buries, where gromwell grows in profusion. They like the hard seeds. The sheep, white and gleaming after shearing, were clustered round Well Cover; the cattle too, kept under the trees. In middle Cover I picked mushrooms and strawberries, and found a solitary frog orchid. I went over to the dewpond and managed to pluck a few water lilies, with the aid of a knife. The stems were thick and slippery, and the water up to my thighs.

June 25

Thunder had cleared the air, so I took an evening bus to Stapleford, and went to Tilsend with my rod. I walked through the garden and field to the riverbank. It was sunny with a cold breeze, and Ibsbury stood out in stark relief, every ditch and fold of down showing up clearly. The Swifts were flying low to drink, and two fat water voles swam up and down finally squeezing themselves into holes between the boards reinforcing the far bank. A Sedge Warbler flew by with a moth bulging from its beak while a Snipe zigzagged overhead drumming. Across the road in the high elms, the Turtle Doves were purring. It really was a super evening. I caught a nice trout of 1 1/2 lbs on a ginger hackle, and threw back a chub and small grayling. On a wire stretched across the Till, perched three baby Swallows, and as I packed up to leave, a White Owl was silently gliding round the meadows.

June 26

A beautiful sunny day! I went from Heytesbury to Sutton Veny across the fields, and climbed up Haycombe, watching the shadows of the clouds as they drifted rapidly over Littlecombe. There were fewer rabbits than usual in the bottom by 'Hammersmith', and dyer's greenweed was growing on the waste ground beside it. There were Wheatears in Long Bottom, and where the various trackways meet, two Turtle Doves were perched on the water trough. On the wood's edge, the turf was made up of coarse wiry grass, yellow rock ose, wild strawberries, and thyme. Lending a spring to the step, and fragrance to the nostrils, the strawberries, hot from the sun, were sweet and delicious to eat.

Along the Roman road, the silver birches cast their shadows across the ferns at their feet. pearl bordered frits, in threes and fours fluttered across the glades, along with a few speckled woods. The rose pink centaury was as its most enchanting, and in some places yellow pimpernel was out in profusion. The bracken reached up to the outspread branches of the dwarf oaks, like a child standing on tiptoe!

June 28

I made my way to Yarnbury from Steeple Langford. A cold wind was blowing but it was sunny and clear. I could pick out the tip of the Cathedral spire, rising up over Fugglestone Down. From Yarnbury's ramparts, the Alton Barnes White Horse was clearly visible above the Pewsey Vale, and I think Huish Hill, also Cold Kitchen, and Cley Hill loomed up beyond Longleat. In front of the earthworks was a field of flax, just blueing up, and rather spoilt by charlock. Walking back along the Stapleford trackway, a Lark flew up from my feet. There under a clod of earth, were four brown eggs, close to the side of the track.

June 30

After biking to Hanging Langford, I walked about Penning's Bottom. A few marbled whites were fluttering around. They lay their eggs on the tall sheeps' fescue grasses, and the caterpillars hatch out in August, feed on their eggshells and then hibernate until December. In that unlikely month they emerge and go on an eating binge until June, when fat and probably comatose, they hang as chrysalis on the fescue grass. The emerging butterflies crawl up the stems to dry their wings, finally appearing in all their black-and-white chequer-board loveliness.

In the Bottom, privet, guilder rose and juniper grow in clumps, along with spindles and buckthorn. There are several large buries there, and rockrose and thyme carpet the moleheaps and anthills. I found a few frog orchids. On the way home, I went to Horsemead and found the Moorhen was sitting on a second clutch of eggs. A Sandpiper flew whistling down stream. It became very cold. A young soldier was fishing Ranks water; he asked me if I belonged to Tilsend? I said, 'No, I just fish here.' He had asked 'the young chappie whether it was all right to fish that water' and been told that no one ever fished that water and he was sure it would be all right. I don't think he caught anything.

July 2

I spent a sunny evening on Ibsbury. It was hazy over the Plain. The yellow and white bedspreads are foaming beside the tracks leading up to the woods. They mingle with pink rest harrow, scabious, knapweed and sanfoin. I hung about the barn watching a Kestrel screaming quite frantically overhead. There were shots from the Down, a man was shooting rabbits, I sat under an oak tree until 9 pm when it started to get damp, and the hares were coming out to feed. On my way down, the sun flowed hazily over the fir plantation, and new Lapwings tumbled in front of me wailing interminably.

July 5

I walked to Shrewton from East Cliffe; a strong wind was blowing off the Plain, bearing the scent of charlock. I stopped to look at a Lark's nest, the bird flew off fluttering a wing, and the eggs are not yet hatched. All the surrounding farms busy haymaking. On the floral scene, St John's wort and knapweed predominate, a tapestry of gold and purple, shot through with the gentle mauve of scabious.

After supper, I canoed down to Wild Duck Island. A Sandpiper led me down the dividing channel between the willow-shrouded islands. Paddling back against the currant, up the main stream, my escort was a Kingfisher. The Green Woodpecker was making a great racket, laughing uproariously! Rain to come!

On June 12th 1948 I left home for Somerset, to work as a student on a mixed farm of 300 acres: all it lacked was sheep. It was situated at Lower Langford on the northern slopes of the Mendips, ten miles from Bristol. The Boss was an an ex-Squadron Leader, not long out of the Air Force, and a tenant farmer on the Wills Estate.

The workforce consisted of a dairyman, a tractor driver, and a good general farm worker. In addition to these, there were three male students, two of them ex-army, the third a 17-year-old fresh from Eton. We were still in that interim period of farming, when both horses and tractors were used though machines were coming in all the time. This farm had a green crop loader for silage making. The dairy herd of 30-40 cows was, as at Petersfinger, predominately dairy shorthorns, plus a couple of high yielding Friesians, and an Ayrshire-shorthorn cross. A bull was kept, called Blazeaway, but recourse was also had to 'The Bull in a Bowler Hat', as the gentleman from the nearby AI Centre was termed, misleadingly, since none of them wore headgear!

We students paid the Boss £5.00 a week, for his tuition, as well as paying for our digs, in a private house, or modest Hotel. Usually I did the afternoon machine milking with Reg the elderly dairyman, one of the old school, who treated his cows individually, knew their little quirks, and how to get the best out of them. For him his cows were not just numbers on an ear tag, but well, cows, to be humoured, and cosseted. If he noticed that the milk yield on a particular day was slightly down, he was not above tipping back his family's ration, in order to top up the last churn. As Cecil the general worker put it, 'Reg do always look to his churns, see.'

All three men were born and bred in the adjacent Chew Valley, and all had the delightful lingual trait of those born in or near Bristol, of appending an 'L' on to words that terminated in the vowels 'A' and 'O'. (Bristol was originally Bristowe!). We talked about areals and good ideals, and quite ordinary boring conversation become memorable, as we talked about my brother in Canadal, and the cricket scores in Australial.. Reference might be made to the childish mischief of our Marial, or Julial. One conversation, admittedly helped along a little in the desired direction, produced the sheer delight of a reference to Gretal Garbol!

I was told some months after my arrival that the men had grumbled at the prospect of working with a female. 'What use will she be to us?' Maybe they had not worked with the Land Girls in the War? I hadn't been long on the farm before I was accepted. We were harvesting, and when they saw that I could load a wagon competently, without help, and that I could keep pace with them at pitching, from 10:30am to 9:30pm, I became accepted as one of the lads. The Boss even went so far as to say to one of them, that I was the best loader of the lot. However, when it came to backing a tractor and trailer, it was a different story. I had no natural aptitude at all.

During the bright, frosty winter days I worked with Arthur, learning the art and skills of hedge laying. He was a master craftsman, and it was a job I enjoyed. At the weekends, I sometimes went home, staying when necessary to help with milking, and on those occasions I would join the men on their Friday evening 'High', a special bus outing to Bristol Speedway at Knowle.

I stayed at Langford until October 1949.

July 31

Returning home for the weekend, I caught the 7:30pm train from TempleMeads to Salisbury. An interminable journey, as we stopped at every little village and halt, and wound our way slowly along the Wylye Valley. The joy of sighting the Westbury White Horse and picking out familiar landmarks, being back on home ground. Tilsend with lights on in the dusk, Horsemead and the rounded slopes of Ibsbury, crowned with the leafy fleece of Grovely.

August 1

I went up to Grovely by Haden Hill, the down now chiefly tinted with the pale mauve of scabious, and the deeper richer, purple mauve of bellflower. There were a few late oxeye daisies, clovers and wild carrot, each saucer-like blossom of the latter sporting at least one orange soldier beetle.

On the banks of the lane climbing up the hill was yellow melilot and the open clearings in the wood smelt deliciously herby, from calamint and wood sage. There were a few marbled whites to be seen, and speckled woods but they weren't in the numbers of last year. I saw a white admiral fly over a privet, and some silver washeds, but clouded yellows which were so abundant last year, were totally absent. Coming down by Ditchampton Farm, a field of oats was being combined.

1949

March 26

I fished at Tilsend; the river was very high. Two Mallard drakes and a duck were flying around, and the water voles were feeding on some weeds. I stopped off at 14 Hatches on the way home, and saw a pair of Kingfishers fly downstream, one behind the other. The water in the Nadder, in contrast to the Wylye, was low.

June 1

I went over to Titchbourne to see how Walt and Doug were getting on. Walt wearing as usual a dazzling white shirt! A wonderful advert for Persil, and a tribute to Mrs Symes dedication! It is about two years since I left, but they had recognised me at some distance, and were genuinely pleased to see me.

Doug had had those bad teeth removed and looked very funny with large gaps. They were cutting the hazels in Clapgates when I joined them. Walt stuttered more than ever from the excitement of my unexpected reappearance on the scene. We had a great talk, and they showed me around. They have some very nice leys of red clover and Italian ryegrass by Studland; some first class wheat, and also some flax, but it was a bit spoilt by charlock. Walt now runs the place, the Boss seldom coming over, except to bring the milk! I stayed to tea with them. Afterwards Bowman looked by. He is very busy with his Pheasant rearing. Walt had a trip of twelve healthy piglets in the sty.

October 10

Anne came with me to see the fungi. It was raining as we walked up the avenue in the rain. We found 25 different species, some of them quite lovely. The only ones I have so far been able to identify, being the deadly death cap, crested *Lepiota*, poisonous *Helvella*, Woolly Milk Cap, and, a query here? either *Russula fragilis*, or *R. emetica*? There were various *Clavaria*, some bright orange, and others white, also a pale yellow and green. They all resembled coral. We also identified blewits and sticky *Volvariella*.

October 12

Ibsbury is full of the most wonderful fungi! I wish I could put a name to them all. Some I found growing on a fallen beech branch, ranging in size from that of a large mushroom to a sixpenny piece. They were white and slightly domed, and they glistened when touched. They were sticky and jelly like, resembling ectoplasm. Underneath, the spores were white and beautifully fluted, and more widely spaced than those of a mushroom. Rabbits were still lying out in the open. It is as warm as midsummer and the leaves show no hint of autumn.

October 17

I walked from Stapleford Castle to Yarnbury. It was squally, with one very heavy shower, which left the sky clear and blue and the visibility good. The sheep were in the middle of the earthwork, and three tractors were busily ploughing about 100 acres of Deptford Down. I lay on the ramparts and watched as they moved along slowly, spaced out, one behind the other as in singling, the soil a beautiful pale fawn with stripes of chalk. A lovely spectacle: the Plain spread out beyond, pale green and grey with a scattering of tree clumps. The sky deep blue with massing banks of white clouds. Going back down the 'Valley of the Shadow', I put up the usual covey of Partridge.

1950

January 19

Alison and I hitched to Tollard Royal, and walked along Ashcombe Bottom. There was a wonderful display of hazel catkins, already fully extended, concertinas of yellow and pink. We startled a Buzzard in the thorn avenue, and it made for the spruce, which stood out darkly against the misty-mazey grey trunks of the bare hazels and limes. The old house had been painted, and the bushes thinned out, reoccupation seems immanent, but nobody was about, so we walked straight through the courtyard and made our way up on to the Ox Drove where the wind was keen. From there we made our way by East Coombe to Ebbesbourne Wake.

January 29

I walked in 'Para' for the first time in months. The fallen and long dead tree, a white poplar that resembled a dragon, has been removed and the canon that overlooked the field of Waterloo has been cut down. There is now a new and flourishing bury in Arcadia. I saw a Green Woodpecker and eight Herons flying over towards the park. On other occasions I have seen as many as thirteen. On my way home I met an old tramp in Boys Meadow. He was making his way to Pewsey, and intending to spend the night in the little copse by High Post. He was much distressed by the loss of his scissors, which a gipsy had stolen from him in Old Sarum Lane!

Early in February I met Shepherd Pierce on the down above Middle Woodford. We talked a little, and liked each other, and when he discovered that I was keen to learn a little about Shepherding, he invited me to come over and help him whenever I wished!

February 12

A sunny frosty morning. I biked over to Lower Woodford to help Shepherd Pierce. I found him busy on Smithen Down. He had 312 Hampshire Down ewes, and lambing was in full swing. The pens were very snug, placed around a central square, which was well strawed down. Each individual pen was backed by straw bales, two deep, and roofed with thatched hurdles. These pens formed the maternity ward for ewes and lambs.

The ewes not yet lambed, are folded 100 yards away, and are let in to fill the square in the evenings. There are many twins, all sooty black. Careful feeding of ewes is vital, since overfeeding results in death. A couple of ewes had lost lambs. Shep skinned these, afterwards tying the skins round one of a pair of twins, and then placing them with bereaved ewes. Should a couple of ewes lamb while he is absent, he can tell which ewe has had twins from the afterbirths. He can see too, the resemblance of the lamb to the parent ewe.

From the pens, we looked away to Woodford with its church and mill, couched under the down, with the blue sky reflected in the Avon curling alongside, and spilling over a little into the water meadows. It looked dreamily peaceful, poised between a perfect glimpse of the Cathedral and Old Serum on the one hand, and over to Durnford Hanging Woods on the other. Shepherd had three dogs with him. I helped with feeding and watering the ewes. He spoke of the wonderful fertility of ground after sheep, and the tragic misuse of 'artificials'. Artificial speaks for itself, 'Muck' is the genuine article.

March 1

Up early, it was misty with a hoar frost, but the sun came out and the day was clear. I joined Shepherd and was on the go all day, but the work was not arduous, and consisted of watering and haying, putting up hurdles, strawing down, and laying straw bundles round the outside of the pens. You cannot leave Hampshire Downs for long while they labour, since the big heads for which they are bred, can make lambing unaided difficult, and in some cases impossible. At the same time, it is important not to help the ewe too soon, in case it strains her.

March 2

Windy with a slight drizzle. There were not very many births in the night. Wally, who is dark and vacant-looking, but a hard worker, and as Shep's governor puts it, 'A halfpenny in the shilling missing,' greeted me with a broad smile, instead of ignoring me as on the previous occasion. He and Shep were watering when I arrived. We lost a lamb. The ewe lambed but couldn't get up, and when we got to the lamb, it was 'drowned', and though Shep blew into its nostrils and mouth, it was too late to revive it. This time Shepherd took the dead lamb, and rubbed it all over one of twins, tying its legs so that it lay and bleated like a new born. The ewe was let into the pen and she accepted the lamb immediately, licking it vigorously. I like Shepherd; he is a great talker and thinking man. He talked of the old times, and told me, 'Never believe there were good old days, they were all very hard for the working man'. His father had brought up a big family on 14 shillings a week, and his grandfather, thirteen children on 10 shillings! He remarked of his own childhood that while they had never starved, because his mother had been a good manager, there was never anything over and to keep the children in shoes had meant constant scrimping. Shepherd seems to be that rare individual who is content with his job. He patently loves it. He can pick out a particular sheep on the down opposite, three-quarters-of-a-mile away, and tell at that distance if a sheep has 'the fly'. A useful tip: if you want to get a ewe to follow you, just carry its lamb by a back leg above the joint, the lamb cries and the ewe follows. Simple! Apparently Shepherd has spoken to his Gov'nor about me, and of how I had looked all over South Wilts for a farm to take me on, and how in the end I had to go for Somerset. The Gov'nor had said, 'What a pity, she'd have done well here'.

In the afternoon the Gov'nor visited the pens and asked me to tea. He and his wife are the real Yeoman stock, and kindness itself. Shepherd speaks most warmly of them both, giving Mrs Edwards the ultimate accolade, of always being 'the first out with her washing'! Meaning, that the poor soul probably rises at 4a.m. to accomplish this feat. I should say that Shep was very loyal in every way. A saying of his is, that 'If a man idles away his Boss' time, he's as good as a thief'.

In the evening, great flocks of Greenfinches descended on the freshly littered pens. Biking home in the dusk, the White Owl was mousing around the Gov'nor's water meadows. He is, I think, the only farmer around here who still digs out his ditches and works the hatches to get the early bite.

March 6

It was sunny with a mist that clung all day to the woods and folds of down. Larks were singing joyously. I have discovered at last what Bakeland is. Shep was talking about the 60 acres, which run alongside the gorse, from Bore Hill to the Turnpike. It was poor land that was let out at a cheaper rate in the old days. Every year it was baked or burnt, but whether the ash was then ploughed in, or how it was done, he could not say. The 60 acres was divided into four plots on a four-year rotation, and each year a quarter was dunged from the winter yard where the heifers were over-wintered. These winter barns were once common on the Plain; sadly many of them are derelict. They were once quite a feature.

Shep, who would never dream of skiving or idling, commented on how many men slack unless the boss is standing by all the time – all due to a 'loss of honesty', and that went for industrial strikers too! I mentioned to him that last summer I had noticed a wonderful rich red hue of the wheat alongside the Turnpike and how alongside that strip, was another piece, that was by comparison, dull and weedy-looking. It goes almost without saying that the rich wheat was grown after sheep, while the other had artificial manure. 'The golden hoof!'

March 6/7

Shep said I might spend a night at the pens, so around 9pm I biked in the dark to Woodford. On the top it was clear, Orion shone brightly through the bare beech

trees, but as I turned off the Turnpike and plunged down Camp Hill, I ran into a
thick mist that had me shivering from the chilling drop in temperature. As I reached
the Foggy Bottom, three Mallards rose up quacking, and disappeared into the
misty meadows.

I spent the best part of an hour with Shepherd and Mrs Pierce in their cottage,
talking and drinking tea. After which he and I walked up on to the down. It was
dark, frosty and starry. There was such stillness in the fold, it was tangible, only
disturbed by the occasional rustle of an uneasy ewe, and a new born lamb keeping
up a persistent bleat. Three ewes lambed while I was there. What hell it must have
been on a wet blustery night, before battery torches, with the lantern perpetually
going out!

A number of planes flew over the Boscombe Down, and the beam of a
searchlight wavered out from the aerodrome. Shep and I leaned against a coop,
and talked, and my eyes kept wandering to Orion and the Pleides, and a beautiful
big red planet, probably Mars that hung low to the East. Talk veered from the evils
of communism, to the rightness architecturally of the flint and stone cottages, and
the death, or near death of Craftsmanship. He expressed admiration for the skills
of those men who had built the Cathedral, and of how today, for all our modern
technical aids we could not equal them. He spoke of how work should be a pleasure,
and of how mechanisation had taken away from men both pleasure and pride in
their skills, which were a matter of self-expression.

He spoke again of his parents in a most endearing way, of how he had
sprung from a humble home, where they had been brought up to be honest. His
parents were devoted, and when his father died, suddenly, at 64 after planting out
potatoes, his mother had followed him four months later, dying of a broken heart.
As he put it, 'She went out like a lamp without oil' (W.H. Hudson mentions this as
happening quite frequently, among simple country folk). Riding home in the dark
in the small hours, there was fog by the Avon farm cottages and first bridge, but
the main bridge and river were clear.

March 8

I woke to hear the Redshanks calling from the meadows; the air was warm and
soft. I decided to visit Titchbourne to see how Walt and Doug were getting on.
There was a profusion of primroses in Clapgates and quite long stalked for early
March. The hurdle maker was at work, close to a keeper's gibbet on which hung,
a Little Owl and three freshly killed Jays, their blue wing bars glinting in the
sunshine. I found Walt dung-carting, and leant him a hand, flinging the loads

straight out on to the ground so that Doug could plough it in. The main news was that one of the under keepers had fought with the head keeper, knocked him out, and been dismissed. A new one had taken up residence in Studland. Two tractors were busy on the neighbouring farms. (Plaskets and Egremonts). I walked back through Batscroft and picked primroses and wild daffs. I caught the bus at Pepperbox.

March 9

Up at 6:15. The sun beginning to disperse the fog in Bemerton but on the Devizes road it was thick and my hair was sopping. The sun tried to come out on Camp Hill but gave up. Shep was pleased and surprised to see me. We were very busy watering and putting hay in cribs and erecting hurdles in the kale and roots for the late lambers due next week. I lambed a ewe on my own. It was quite simple. Always pull the lamb round towards the udder, to avoid straining the ewe. Today triplets were born, all very small. Shep told me that his father used to plough with an ox team.

Later in the afternoon I biked to the Richmond's at Netherhampton for tea. On the way I watched a pair of Moorhens drinking in the muddy channel that runs alongside the Netherhampton road. They looked so spick and span with black glossy coal grey front and red and yellow beak and that finishing touch of white wing feather.

March 10

The lambing pens again, a cold grey day, and windy. We lunched in the shelter of Shep's hut, and discussed Landlords Past and Present! In Shep's experience, whilst landlords today, won't do repairs, or put in flush lavatories for their workers, it is because they can't afford to. Before the War, when they could have done so, they often wouldn't.

Shep's father had been shepherd to the Hon Greville for 30 years at Heale. Shep had worked there too. 'The man had been so mean', he said, 'that if lambing had been going on in a blizzard, he would send the Shepherd, just half a dozen lumps of coal for his fire!' Shep had left his service, 'Because I didn't care for the man', and thereupon Greville had turned round and sacked his father, the old man who had served him so faithfully for so long. In the meantime Shep had found himself a job with a builder, but he immediately left it in order to find his father another shepherding post, and then had stayed to help him with it. Thereby taking, as he expressed it, 'an Irishman's rise'.

We had a ewe in difficulty, the lamb was coming tail first, and it was 'a twinner'. Shep thought that he would have to turn it, but mercifully he managed to get the legs out. He looked up at me with a merry twinkle in his eye, and said, 'I prayed before that one', adding, 'My Mother's dying words were, Sid put your trust in the Highest of all!' He continued, 'I always felt she wouldn't have said it, if she hadn't believed it to be true, and the best thing'.

April 5

Alison and I went to Salisbury Races for the first time in our lives! We biked to the Race Plain. I was pleased to find that I could still get up to the fork without dismounting. In the evening we went into the first field and picked green withy wands for Aunt N. The kingcups were out. We stood by the island fence and admired the Cathedral. Now often one takes it for granted, just seeing it without consciously appreciating that vast stone miracle growing upwards out of the meadows. We saw the first Reed Bunting back and the Snipe were drumming. Now that evenings are drawing out the big boys wander into the second field and beyond nesting.

April 9

The sun came out about 10am. It was very sultry. I hiked over to the Pennings near Turnpike, and found Wally and old Kyte picking up cribs. Two of the young Kytes were working nearby, one ploughing, and the other discing. As a family they are quite a tribe. Some of the little ones have the most gorgeous hair, not ginger but copper coloured. Collectively they are know in the village as 'the little copper knobs!'

Shep was putting up hurdles, and the ewes are now folded on rye and clover. Rye is not particularly good for sheep, but is used as a stopgap until the grass is ready. There are now 322 lambs, and a few more still to come. They have grown a lot since my last visit, and look very well. Shepherd advised me that were I to keep sheep, I should buy in tegs at August Fair, sell in November, at the same time buying in again to sell in March then again buy in at the same time, to sell again in the August. Probably the most trouble-free way of keeping sheep, and a means of acquiring ready cash.

Some land is too rich for sheep, but they will do well on it for three months. Lambs on the same land will thrive for a few weeks and then die.

April 24

Spring has come with a sudden rush; the violets and primroses are giving way to cowslips and stitchwort. I found our white speckled Blackbird's nest in the laurel in front of the variegated maple. The Sedge Warblers are churring in the meadows and as usual there is a Wren's nest in the old pollard willow by Spring Bridge.

April 25

I listened to a Blue Tit singing in the old crab tree in the garden, which has blossomed so beautifully, the more so for having been severely pruned last autumn. As I write this in bed it is snowing hard! The flakes gleam like silver in the lamplight.

April 26

I wake up to find heavy snow. It is quite odd to see from my window green willows standing in white fields with the white Race Plain beyond.

April 27

Alison and I hitched to Tollard Royal and walked along the track to Ashcombe Bottom, where a white poplar with bursting buds was backed by a screen of pale green elm seeds. We lunched under a blossoming crab tree just below the house where the carpets of primroses were almost over. In Ashcombe Bottom we watched a pair of Marsh Tits pulling strips of lichen off an ash tree. The sycamores were particularly spectacular, the ledges on the lower part of the trees were bronze, the dangling florets not yet turned yellow, and the unopened buds at the tops clustered and pink reflected the sunshine.

Poor Ali suddenly started 'Charlotte' (period pains): she was in agony. I had to help her up to the caretaker's house in the old stables. The Harleys were away, so I used their phone to ring for a 'Sand Car' (taxi) to come from Sarum to fetch us! An hour-and-a-half passed and no sign of one. I was pleased to see inside Cecil Beaton's Ashcombe and liked what the Caretaker showed me. Then I climbed up the slope just in time to see a car disappear along the Ox Drove! The downs were verdant green with streaks of snow lingering in the gullies. The 'Sand Car' reappeared and we headed for home.

In the evening I went birds'-nesting with Raymond (a twelve-year-old village boy). We found a Redshank's nest with three eggs in the usual field near the wooden bridge. A pair of Plovers was circling round low, crying, but we failed to locate the nest. Raymond shinned up an oak tree to look at a Crow's nest but it proved to be empty. We walked on into 'Para' to the 'Tree of Life' field; from there you can see no sign of sprawling Sarum, just green fields, willows and streams. Raymond is a very unusual boy of his class, sensitive and very intelligent. He deplored the new estate now spreading over the Tournament down. He said 'What a lovely cornfield it had been and what fun he had had playing in the stubble'.

We went on towards the Netherhampton road and in the marshy field from Redshanks rose up together. Plovers were very excited but we found no nests. We went home over the bridge by the little fir plantation. Later I found a Chaffinch nest with four eggs in the Squarey's garden.

April 28

Raymond and I biked to Stratford and Little Durnford meadows. We found a Mallard's nest in a pollard willow with eight eggs, a Bullfinch in a willow stump, a White Owl flying around, a snipe drumming. Later Raymond found an Owl sitting on Jackdaw's eggs in 'Para'.

May 7

Dull cold and wet. How I loathe a wet May. It's a sort of blight and is wasting my last free summer on the downs and in the woods. The meadows are as soggy as in mid-winter. I went over to Wallmead Farm with Mrs Tilden to visit Jack and Daisy Shallcross. Daisy is Kitty's older sister. After inspecting their piglings, and tea, Jack, Mike Rawlence, Sid and I paced the bounds of the farm. Tisbury parish church bells were ringing and the sun came out for a short while. It's lovely how the church is almost in the fields. The may was out in Wallmead copse.

One of the fields had a lot of iron stone in it. I think these are pyrites. Two of the piglets are to be a wedding present to me and Kit!*

May 9

I spent the morning and afternoon with Shepherd, at the Pennings. There was a hot breeze, but it was an easy day for us. The old ewes were looking very tatty; they will soon be shorn. The lambs were folded on vetches that were full of corn cockle. We turned the ewes out into Pennings Bottom, and mended the gaps in the fences to keep them out of the corn after shearing. Haymaking is in full swing, three ricks are up already. Behind the eaten vetch, the ground is very flinty. Until the War the ground had never been ploughed. Before I left, the dogs drove the sheep to water.

I had become engaged in January, and my husband-to-be had gone on with other older ex-service students to the Royal Agricultural College at Cirencester after completing his year of practical farming at Lower Langford. We had planned to marry in August, and during his holiday breaks we were desperately looking for a farm in South Wilts. At that time few came on the market and those that did were too large for novices, or too expensive. In the end we had to settle for a farm at Nempnett Thrubwell in North Somerset, on the lower slopes of the Mendips, overlooking Blagdon Reservoir. This for me terminated an intense 'love affair' with South Wiltshire, and it took quite a bit of coming to terms with. It was a very busy time; the farmhouse needed a great deal done to it, and an eye needed to be kept on the various workmen involved. At home our aged gardener, an ex Marine who had once served on the Royal Yacht, and loved to spin yarns about King 'Teddy' (Edward VII) could just about manage the vegetables. I looked after the large Herbaceous borders. My Aunts were getting old, and my special one was not well enough to cope with all the wedding preparations. As a result I found myself seeing to wedding invitations, caterers, hiring of marquees, bridal attire, bridesmaids' dresses and flowers, and at the same time making sure that I made the most of my last few months in the Wiltshire countryside.

May 10

I biked to the Great Yews via Odstock. Leaving my bike there, I climbed the steep hill to where the road ended by a wood. It was a sunny day with a still breeze. The yews are said to be prehistoric, and they certainly look it. They are well off the beaten track, and to walk beneath their massive trunks and to experience their still aura of sanctity is a similar feeling to that produced by the nave of a great cathedral. A century or more ago, sheep stealers sought sanctuary beneath their branches; only an occasional column of smoke billowing upwards, might betray their presence to the rare passer by. The Swiss chalet in the middle clearing, was deserted but in good repair. It was erected by the Radnor's and is said to be haunted, but I have never sensed anything there. On the north-west side of the wood, surrounded by thorn bushes, spindles and big yew, there is a lovely sunny glade, full of flowers, bees and butterflies and the yew branches sweep the ground. There is a haunted glade where no birds ever sing and there I never linger, always having a feeling of unease.

In yet another glade I watched the first Flycatchers perform their aerobatics for my delight. There were orange tip butterflies fluttering about the brambles, and speckled woods were on the ash flowers. I walked along Grims Ditch, with the intention of visiting the Nightingale copse on Black Down, but idling awhile under a hawthorn where tracks cross, I looked up suddenly to see this ghostly looking little old man, with a walking stick, moving silently towards me. There in the emptiness he appeared spectral, quite unreal. 'Good Afternoon', I said. He removed his hat in a most courtly manner, bowing slightly, then came and sat beside me on the bank.

An hour-and-a-half passed, and he never drew breath, talking in a quiet manner about many things. His speech was full of archaisms from a century ago. I wondered if he might be a little bit touched, not in an unkind way, but in the same way that some interesting people can appear a little mad, because their thoughts are not run-of-the-mill, or those of the common herd. He began by remarking, 'You are very brave to come out here alone'. 'I don't think so, I like being alone'. I told him that I was listening out for Nightingales. 'I don't think that you will hear them here,' he said, adding that I should try Grovely on the Barford side of the Race Plain. He was, he said, 85 years old, and he claimed to still walk 20 or 40 miles a day. He was a born Wiltshire man. 'Nowhere to compare with South Wilts.' 'Did I know Grovely? It was more lovely than Whitsbury Down.' (Agreed!) Somehow we got on to the subject of gipsies. 'How very singular that you should mention them! I am a naturalist, psychologist and student of human nature, and I have noticed and told ladies and gentlemen and ordinary people, that gipsy girls never philandered outside their race!' I remarked that Borrow too, had said something of the sort. I mentioned Kit, my fiancé, and thereafter he referred to him, as my 'young gentleman'.

I discovered that he had lived? (lodged?) in Bemerton, and appeared to know everyone including the Aunts by sight. He also claimed to know old Bennet Stanford, the late Archie Morrison, and Lord Pembroke's father. He thought Lady Pembroke, 'A direct woman, who spoke as she thought!' Adding, 'Do not get the impression that I know her, I mean only that I am acquainted with her.' He walks mostly at night, and in the early morning, 'to observe natural phenomena'. He claimed to be psychic (which didn't surprise me) and sees more than meets the eye. At the moment he is lodging at Little Toyd Farm. I walked with him past the yews again, and we parted on the hill. He wished me luck and expressed the hope that in a few years time, we might find a permanent farm in Wiltshire. I shall never forget his face as he sat beside me in his mac and old hat, his white hair, lined forehead, bright eyes and moustache, saying most emphatically, 'People are wrong. There is no sin, only ignorance!' This said, he turned and quickly merged into the landscape. Who on earth was he? We said we would meet again, perhaps in Grovely Woods?

I biked home by Coombe Bisset, and the Race Plain. Coming down the far side, just before the Netherhampton fork, I heard 'jug, jug' and dismounted to listen to a Nightingale, its tone almost strident, such piercing volume, and finally those clear liquid, breath stopping notes.

May 17

I woke at 6am, sun pouring in at my window. A Garden Warbler singing in the variegated maple, a Greenfinch 'dweeing', Goldfinches twittering. After supper I biked to the Race Plain, the may was fully cut, and Nightingales were in full-throated song in the copse and there was just a little song from the Hare Warren. I came back along the Netherhampton–Sarum road, and walked about the marshy field where the six ponies graze. There among some rushes and coarse grass, I found a Yellow Wagtail's nest. Great excitement, as it was the first I had found! The hen flew off as I approached, and there were six brown eggs. I came home through Sarum; the Swifts were flying low, fairly swooping down Fisherton Street.

May 18

It was sunny and breezy. I was up for 6am, and went straight into the water meadows. The may was fully out in the second field, the three outstanding trees were loaded, one white, the second off-white faintly tinged with pink, and the third is a strawberry and cream pink.

In the afternoon I went to Steeple Langford, and on to the down by Cliffe Farm. The may in blossom along the track, also a big patch of star of Bethlehem halfway up. I watched the Wheatears on the down above the covers, and a pair was nesting beside the old milestone at Yarnbury. Milkwort was out and the early orchises, also 'eggs and bacon' and squinancywort. I came down by the old castle and bussed home.

After supper I biked to Barford St Martin, and walked to Grovely. There were no Nightingales singing, only Garden Warblers and Blackbirds. I walked about enjoying the bluebells, yellow archangel, and woodruff, the may on the outskirts, and the pale amber of the oaks. All the time rain threatened. Walking back over Barford down in the dusk, I put up a Stone Curlew; with a loud 'curlee' it flew off low towards the wood, its' double white wing bars outstanding in the gloom.

The cow parsley frothing round the base of the 13th Earl on his plinth among the lime trees outside Wilton House, had just been scythed. Also that along the Wishford Lane, always rather saddening, a sign that peak growth had been reached, and soon haymaking must follow.

May 19

It was dull and cold all day. About 6pm, I biked out beyond Wishford and walked across the meads to Horseman Hatch, and then towards Hanging Langford. Apart from the early kingcups, the charm of these meadows lies chiefly in their overgrown hedgerows, tall willow trees and the seasonal birds of passage.

May 20

In the evening I climbed up to Ibsbury, through a blaze of buttercups, daisies, saxifrage, and wheeling Plovers. It was a sunny evening. I did the round through the wood. There were hundreds of baby rabbits, I sat on the earthwork until the babies came out and sat like little statues, noses twitching. The scent of bluebells wafted out of the wood, and on to the downs. They grow unrivalled under beech trees; under oaks there is competition from dog's mercury and nettles.

May 21

Raymond (a village boy of 12) and I looked at a Kestrel's nesting site, in the old quarry by the Whiting Works. It was unreachable, as were several Jackdaws. We found a Whitethroat's nest in some brambles at the base. Later I found a Greenfinch's nest in a yew at the Squareys; they build in it every year. I watched the Sand Martins flying low over the river, As always they are nesting in the drainpipes in the riverbank of the croquet lawn. The parent birds fly in and out, and the young's first flight risks the peril of drowning, but as far as I know they never do.

May 22

Raymond and I biked to the Race Plain, and found a Willow Wren's nest among the brome grass. Also several Whitethroats. We went a little way along the 'Old Coach Road' and searched the adjacent woods. A Nightingale sang in a copse, and there was a marvellous scent of herbs. Rhododendrons were in flower, and the wild raspberriess soon will be. On Hunt's Down some very quizzy yearlings followed us and we caught a glimpse of the keeper with dog and gun, lurking in the shadow of the Hare Warren.

May 23

I hiked to Stockton; it was dull and rather cold. I walked up to the Great Ridge from Stratton's Farm. The sheep on Stockton Down were clustered around and under the 'umbrella tree', an old beech that provides the only shade available. I dipped down the right-hand slope between the junipers, and perched on the edge of a small quarry, where innumerable small rabbits were milling about. I then followed the track on into the wood until I hit the Roman road. There had been a lot of tree felling since my last visit. I turned off along the narrow trail that runs parallel with it because from there it is possible to fully appreciate the sheer splendour of the bluebells, stretching as they do into seeming infinity among the ferns and scrubby dwarf oaks, with here and there clumps of meadow saffron. The Nightingales, Whitethroats and Blackcaps were in full voice. I watched a Tawny Owl perched against the trunk of one of the taller oaks, blending with its lichened trunk and the leaf shadow. He sat boldly upright, regarding me through deceptively sleepy eyes. He was aware of every movement!

Rain was all around, black clouds blotted out Win Green, and the closer Fonthill Ridge. Only a few drops reached me and I was turning off down the Roman snail bank into Longdean Bottom, where I saw a few little roe deer. Stoney Hill is now down to ley, and had a nice bite of grass that hid the multitudes of flints that gave rise to its name. The usual masses of yellow charlock festooned the edge of the long, long, field that runs alongside the endless boring stretch to Stockton Railway Bridge.

May 26

I biked to Laverstock with Philip Glasier (Falconer and Bird Photographer). We abandoned our bikes to climb the down, which was spangled with assorted orchids, bee, fragrant, and pyramidal. We went a little way along the vallum, and then over to East Plantation, where Philip had the misfortune to tread on a Partridge chick – that is to say it was unfortunate for the chick! The plantation was full of Pigeon, but we saw no Sparrow Hawks, the object of our walk, although we heard them screaming. It is a very long plantation and Philip with his irons, shinned up dozens of firs and larches looking for nests. We found only one – a Kestrel with five eggs, a late clutch.

May 27

I went to Bowerchalke and up Church Bottom on to the Ox Drove. Among a tangled growth of long grass and robin-run-the-hedge, I found a pretty little nest at eye level. It was domed and mostly made of moss, plus a little grass, and a few twisty fibres woven into the entrance. There were no eggs, and no sign of birds. Probably a Chaff-Chaff's, but it could be a Willow Wren, though they usually nest on the ground, but not invariably. Further up the drove, in a tangle of wild rose, was a Hedge Sparrow with four blue eggs. I ended up on Marley Combe, where there were plentiful Wheatears and rabbits. The two go together.

In the evening I took Kit to see the Yellow Wagtail's nest. The eggs are not yet hatched. We found a Morhen's nest under brambles overhanging the stream. Beautifully made of hay, very neat, the tidiest I have seen. It contained seven eggs.

From a nearby nest eight young Morhen chicks had just emerged. The mother ran up the steep bank, and one of the chicks got left behind. Each time it tried to climb it fell back into the water. I waded across and so to say, gave it a leg up!

May 28

Philip's asked me to join him in looking for Hobbies. We biked along the Turnpike as far as Diment's, but the firs were too small for a Hobby's liking. Again the ground was moving with rabbits. Col.Bailey's men were busy haymaking on Normanton Down. On Wilsford Down we came across a poaching black cat dragging along a rabbit almost as big as itself. It emerged from a covert just as we were entering it, and at the same moment a Sparrow Hawk flew past us at some speed.

May 30

In the evening I biked along the Turnpike above Hooklands. Whitethorn scented the open Bakeland. The Plovers were wheeling and tumbling. I found one youngster couched by a hammock, among the buttercups and salad burnet. At my approach it ran away, all legs and speckles, and the parent birds very agitated.

May 31

I took Philip to see the Yellow Wagtails; the young had hatched and he and Bernard Jeans were anxious to photograph them. We went on to the Quarry above Tinkerpit, to see how accessible the Kestrel's nest might be from the beech grove at the top. Arriving there, Philip clapped his hands and the echo sent the hen flying off into a nearby tree. From there she regarded us as we surveyed the scene. It proved impossible to reach the nest without a rope. Philip placed a small mirror on the end of a stick, and lowered it. We could see the young, apparently newly hatched: yellowish, tinged with fluff, heads a-flopping. There appeared to be only two. There was also a Great Tit's nest in a hole half way up the cliff, and a Stock Dove sat on eggs on a ledge.

June 1

It was a supremely lovely day, hot and sunny. After doing the household shop, I leapt on my hike and was away to the Race Plain. Along the road bank of the Hare Warren the wild strawberries were quite ripe. At the top I stopped to listen to a Nightingale singing from the top of a hazel, quite oblivious of me. I went along the Coach Road, the may now a little past and over, but the elders were just beginning to flaunt their chaliced lace. A little short of Chislebury, I stopped to eat my sandwiches and admire the view over towards Grovely. Suddenly, on looking up, I saw that two Willow Wrens in the may tree under which I was sitting, were becoming increasingly agitated. One had an insect in its beak. I poked around and found the nest among the tussocks of pale green rough grass. The young were just hatched. I moved further along so that I could watch without disturbing them.

I then moved on to Chislebury, and walked about the rings, which were clothed in milkwort, buttercups, saxifrage, salad burnet and 'eggs and bacon'. After which I sped on to Fovant Hut, that whitewashed grey-tiled cottage, the only habitation on the ten-mile stretch, then on down the hill to Alvediston.

Cruising through the leafy tunnel, high banked with ferns and trailing ivy, that leads to Berwick St John, I met a pony trap. It was coming towards me at a spanking pace, driven by two elderly gipsy women, their brown lined faces set off by gay red spotted turbans. They wore gauzy blouses and high-waisted skirts that shored up their ample breasts, and of course dingle-dangle earrings. 'Can you tell us the time, my lady?' On the side of the trap was painted, 'Georgina Cooper, Yeovil'. They let me take their picture, and tried to sell me a scrubbing brush!

It was by now very hot as I pushed my bike up the long steep twisty lane that leads so Winkelbury, and on past the windbreak of firs and sycamores, that run beside the Ox Drove. I stopped and walked over to the big beech clump. It was wonderfully clear over towards Rushmore, the Chase and the Blue Beyond. The curlews were calling from Malacombe Bottom. I took a few photos of Ashcombe and Win Green, and then the damned shutter went and stuck, and nothing would shift it!

Above Ashcombe the ground was mossy, warm form the sun, and soft to bare feet. Beyond the beeches it was flinty, and far down below in the garden of Ashcombe House a man was digging the garden. I lay for a while under the beech clump, listening to the wind soughing in the leaves, and watching the white clouds drifting over Win Green. All among the fragrant thyme and wiry herbage were little black iridescent beetles with red heads, and fluttering orange tip butterflies and green hairstreaks.

Back again on the Ox Drove the tarmac soon gave out, and the going became difficult. It was perfect photographic weather, and turning a corner there was the perfect picture, and, my camera shutter refused to function! Tethered beside the drove were six piebald ponies, and two mongrel dogs. Outside two gaily-painted vans, two small children played. A small boy and a little girl with gingery curls wearing a pink dress, both filthy but healthy looking. There were hens and day-old chicks in a coop under the hedge and an excited puppy of mixed parentage. A seedy man appeared and my two women of the morning! Great excitement as they recognised me. Me cursing internally that my shutter was jammed, and of course by tomorrow they would be miles away! Even up there, apparently, they were moved on pronto. A little further on where the path widened out, I met a small girl leading a grey pony, and several small boys, about five in all; adorable little urchins! Gipsy children are attractive but age makes them grow furtive and deceitful. A pity but hardly surprising, seeing the way they are chivvied about. Their rags were strewn all over the bushes, as Matthew Arnold put it so colourfully, 'Every bush I see, with scarlet patches tagged and shred of grey…'

At that end of the Ox Drove the may is still at its best. Wild roses adorn the hedges and honeysuckle buds are near bursting. Kestrels hung overhead as I sped down Church Bottom, the evening sun lengthening the shadows of the thorn bushes. Signs of haymaking in progress. The grass lay in swathe on several farms along the drove. Reaching the bottom I stopped for a paddle in the cool water of the Ebble where it runs beside the peaceful road.

June 4

It has been another very hot day and while musing on the iron bridge opposite Cooks Farm I saw a Little Owl fly into a willow. I found the nest in a hole only four feet from the ground. Inside were two young owlets, feathers just bursting from the quills, hissing madly.

After tea I biked over to the Harnham meadows to peek at the Yellow Wagtails. Philip and Bernard, who had set up a hide, were just packing up. They had taken good shots of the cock who had flown in and perched on a stick that they had placed close to the nest for that purpose. The hen had preferred to approach by running through the grass. After packing up they biked back with me to Cook's Bridge, and I showed them the Little Owl's nest. They decided to set up a hide there. They wanted me to go on with them to Pitton to look for Sparrow Hawks, but I had to refuse as I was going out to supper.

Philip has confirmed my sightings over the years of Sandpipers at Wild Duck islands. The local Birdmen had pooh-poohed him! Silly idiots! Why don't they look for themselves? It's the perfect site for them.

June 5

I walked along to look at the Little Owl, and discovered a Green Woodpecker's hole in a willow in the same field and about ten feet up. I heard the young chirruping and the old bird laugh inside. 'Snake Bird' seemed very appropriate naming when she came out, slowly wriggling because the hole was tight. A pair of Kingfishers are nesting on the island opposite and are going back and forth all the time. I met up with Philip and Bernard, who had been at the hide since the small hours, taking shots of the Little Owls at 4:30am! They too had spotted the Kingfishers, and found a Greater Spotted Woodpecker's nest close by in Boys Meadow Copse. The golden flax irises are out along the riverbanks, and several hatches of baby ducklings were on the water. A flycatcher has built in the creeper above the dining room window, and a pair of Bullfinches were pecking away at the gravel in front of the house.

June 9

After supper, I biked to Wishford, and walked about Kingsmead and along both banks of the river. The flag irises were spectacular, and little clouds of gnats were eddying up over the ragged robin and buttercups. Coming back in the dusk, I spied Philip on the bridge, so stopped and we talked awhile. Bernard was in the hide; the Owl came twice to the young while I was there. She visits every ten minutes or so, from 9:45pm, until 11:30pm. After that there are no more visits until dawn. As bulbs flashed Philip ran up with new ones. On the bridge, the only sounds were the odd duck quacking, the creaking tit-a-tit of a Moorhen, and the kwonging of a Coot, while all the time the mist curled up from the river face and the air grew chill.

June 10

I met Philip punctually at 8:30pm on the bridge. We then pinpointed the Kingfisher's nest on the island to the left of an alder. The Little Owls flew in promptly at 9:30pm and visited regularly until about 11pm when they finished. The cows were browsing noisily around the hide, the cowie smell of their breath, intensified by dewfall and the damp mist from the river. There was a scattering of summer stars. A swan and cygnets sailed serenely by, without so much as a hiss from the cob bringing up the rear. The fish were rising at 10:30 with satisfying plops. It would appear that Little Owls do not roost with their young, once they are feathered up.

June 12

Philip and I made for the Quarry, to see if we could reach the young Kestrels with a fishing net. The nest has three entrances: the first and third were in line, the second was in between and slightly below. Poking with a long beech branch proved ineffective; we will try again with a rope. Meantime we went over to the island and fixed a post in the middle of the river, opposite the nest. Then we cut back all briars and possible Kingfisher perches, and made a clearing in the nettles for the hide.

It struck me that bird photographers, if not very careful must make a lot of birds desert. Philip admitted that there must be very few that hadn't without actually admitting that he had. Personally I would rather just watch them. We looked at the Green Woodpeckers and found they had flown. At dusk, the Cuckoo called, and noctule bats were flitting over the river.

June 15

I took the bus to Norton Bavant and walked up to Scratchbury. The track is overhung by scycamores, which have the largest and finest wings I have ever seen. They were just turning pink. I lay on the vallum and looked over to North Farm. The intermediate down was sprinkled with sweet scented fragrant and palmate orchids. Way ahead I could see the battle-scarred clump of trees on the Imber road. Battlesbury and Longleat woods were to the west also the redbrick School of Infantry which intrudes but not too rudely. I climbed the down and walked by fields of barley to East Hale (a farm hamlet). Up the hill beyond that to the fit plantation, on the edge of which a lot of rabbit snares had been set. Then over Knook down for a little while in the direction of Chitterne. I turned back along the wind break, the wind sighing in it like the sea. On Knook Down I lay and watched a thin line of Aberdeen Angus cattle straggling along. Quaking grass and lady slipper were abundant. I went past Upton Great Barrow and explored a larch plantation for Sparrow Hawks and then came down to Codford St Peter and paddled in the stream at Sherrington.

June 19

While I was forking over a rose bed a hen Blackbird hopped within a few feet of me and then made a quick grab at a caterpillar between my feet. Its beak at the time, already crammed with five or six assorted grubs! Philip looked over and we tried for the Kestrels again, calling in on Dennis Squarey on the way to borrow a rope. This Philip tied securely round a beech tree at the quarry's edge, and made fast the loose end around his waist. He lowered himself over, kicking down the loose chalk as he went. After a few minutes, he handed me up two fledglings, one for Bill (his wife) and one for me, and an unexpected third was left for the birds.

They had the most beautiful green eyes, and pale yellow feet. Their heads and backs were still downy.

June 20

I was up at 6am and biked along the Wishford Lane. There, under the tall elms, I saw two dark shapes. One was a cock Blackbird, ticking madly at a young Little Owl, which had fallen from the nest. I picked it up, and carried it with me up Hadden Hill to Grovely. The mist was stirring round Ibsbury, and it lay in thick pools over Wishford; here and there patches of sunshine broke through over the woods. After breakfast Dennis came over with a freshly killed mouse for the Kes; I have named her Jill. She ate the tail half, and some raw meat. At the moment I am keeping her in the old stable, along with Minerva, the Little Owl. Initially Jill hissed at her, but they are now sitting happily together. Meantime Philip is making them both perches.

June 22

I am receiving fairly regular offerings of mice and beetles, which go down well with both birds. The odd worm goes down well with Minerva and Jill enjoying fresh rabbit, chopped, and with the fur left on. Philip and I biked out to Berwick St James, and walked up the woody slope to Asserton looking for Hobbies. No joy. We came back along the Turnpike, turning off down the hill to Stoford. The hay had been lifted from the big field around the beech clump. It had, before mowing, been aglow with poppies.

July 1

Drove to Stourhead with Mrs Tilden, Kitty and Sid. Last time I was there, was as a child of 11 for a Boxing Day meet outside the house. I remember the stirrup cup going round. I had never seen the gardens before.

We drove through the Nadder Valley, Hindon and Mere. It was my first meeting with Sid. He is a Jew boy from the East End and like Kitty highly intelligent and stuffed with brains, but from a widely disparate background. I liked him very much but think he is probably a Commie, very red anyway!

Astounding place! Stourton village was full of trippers picnicking on the strip of green before the Gothic church. The grounds are perfect in their way. As we strolled along, Sid started yowling about exploited labour and the waste of money. I said I thought it likely Henry Hoare's labourers were grateful for a steady wage to take home to their large and hungry families, but who knows! I added that, to create beauty was never a waste, and thank God England was not yet quite reduced to rows of uniform bungalows, and that Henry had a perfect right to build as he pleased. He must have employed hundreds.

Kitty and I enjoyed the peace and quiet of nature in its contrived setting, but Sid was decidedly oppressed by the thought of so much money expended on classical architecture, pantheons and temples of gods and goddesses, grottos and nymphs and artificial lakes! He really had it in for Henry!

My feeling was, that creating such a beautiful landscape for posterity to enjoy, long after his body has crumbled to dust, was a considerable achievement. According to my Bradley and Hutton, which I perused last night, the famous Bristol Cross was 'given' to Henry Hoare by, of all people, a clergyman. It was a virtual theft from the city of Bristol, to whom it belonged. Apparently Henry Hoare had a propensity for 'appropriating such unconsidered trifles'. It has to be said, this was a rather large one!

I told Kitty and Sid about a former owner, Lord Stourton, having been hung in Salisbury by a silken cord, a privilege granted to erring noblemen. In his case, for murdering an equally nasty father and son. Stourton's accomplices in this foul deed, were hung in chains in Mere, all this in the reign of Bloody Mary.

Drove home via Sedgehill, Semley and Donhead on to the Shaftesbury road. We ended up at Chiselbury at sunset. The barley in the centre scintillated pink and mauve like shot silk. Kitty told us it had been built by the Beaker folk as an enclosure for cattle. We walked round the vallum. Profusion of orchids, bee, fragrant and pyramidal.

July 24

We searched for Sparrow Hawks in Pitton and Farley woods, but the woods are too big. We started our search near Alderbury, where we combed the first fir wood after the keepers' cottage. In it we found dead man's bones, that weird fungus that starts like a glossy egg, then from that, out of it bursts a jelly substance, and from that again springs a white horn that is pitted in much the same way as an old bone. The horn is surmounted by a cap and it smells awful!

The plantations are well managed and preserved. Branches hang low, and cover every inch of ground. As for Sparrow Hawks, we drew a blank every time. We had no compensation for emerging dusty and dirty and covered with pine needles. Next, we tried Nightwood Copse, which in contrast to the murk and bareness of the pine woods, flaunted great patches of colour, from pink pools of centaury, yellow St John's wort and dyers greenweed. Again no sight or sound of hawks. Biking on through Pitton and Farley, we stopped off at all woods en route. Heading towards the London Road, one pinewood looked ideal, but proved blank, except for a Little Owl. We emerged on to a piece of down, where firs had been felled, and the ground was a carpet of golden moss and rockrose, and from among the buries and tree stumps, we flushed a Stone Curlew.

Philip is dark haired and stocky, very serious and smiles but seldom. When talking of his army days, it was obvious he had been a bit of a maverick: it was no surprise! I am amused by, and quite like, the 'good trooper' attitude he adopts towards me on expeditions. As I am to be away for a few days, he offered to look after Jill and Minerva. I gratefully accepted; two more birds cannot make much difference! He is already looking after 'Jaal' (a friend's Goshawk), also Diana Dunn's Goshawk that arrived while she was in Scotland. In addition, he has his own Merlin, Bill's Kestrel, plus two ducks, and two more Goshawks are arriving at any moment. The perching problem must be acute! The tiny house is bursting at the seams, with dogs and three babies.

On my way home across 'Broken Bridges', a Redshank flew up out of the water lane that runs beside the footpath. It shot past me whistling, disappearing momentarily into the withey bed, then flew back again to perch on a dead thorn beside the raised footpath. From there it gave vent to an angry alarm note. I dismounted to look for the young, which I knew must be close by in the long grass or brambles. No sign, but my aunt passing by with the dogs half an hour later saw them couched beside the path.

July 19

After a hot sweaty day in London, Alison and I went over to the Squarey's at 8pm and swam in the river, which is higher than for some time. Three baby Sand Martins shot out from one of the drainpipes, and just missed being swept away by the current. The last slanting rays of sunshine were glancing down the river and midges were dancing at the water's edge. We looked for crayfish, turning over the stones as in our childhood, holding them up between thumb and forefinger, firmly between the joints, so that they could not nip as they wriggled and twisted. When released, they shot off backwards, propelled by their fanlike red tails. We caught instead, the speckled 'hammerheads' in our cupped hands. All head and tail, they rest inertly on the stony bottom, blending so well as to be almost invisible. They are often called 'Miller's Thumbs, because the old timemMillers were supposed to develop broad thumbs, from their habit of rubbing the grain between thumb and forefinger. It was fun! We came out glowing after half an hour.

July 20

Bernard drove Philip and me over to Bulford, to look at the Hobby's nest, which had been robbed last year. It was on War Department land. We followed the course of the Eight-Mile River on to Milston Down, where there are lots of little fir and spruce plantations dotted about in straggling and irregular shapes. The tall grasses had gone to seed, and the ragwort had been completely stripped of flower and foliage by the cinebar caterpillars. Bernard, having located the wood, sent Philip to walk around the outside of it, while he and I walked straight to the nesting site. A young Lesser Spotted Woodpecker flew screaming around us as we walked.

Meanwhile an army truck had bumped its way across the down towards us. Three men with dogs jumped out and followed us, and as they closed the gap, they challenged us. Bernard in his slow unhurried way explained who he was, and that we were bird photographers. Thereupon the younger man, who was very pucka, and of the old brigade, expressed his delight; he had feared that with climbing irons and binoculars, we were up to no good. He introduced himself as being Capt Compton of the Bulford and Tidworth Syndicate. It ended with him telling us, that he had seen a Hobby screaming overhead in Bedlam Wood, which is just over the Hampshire border above Shipton Bellinger. He gave us full details.

The two men accompanying him were keepers, both nice, the elder tall and moustached. They had several dogs with them, fleet of foot, and a glorious red, they looked like a greyhound – retriever cross. While we watched, one of them ran down two rabbits, which were given to me. The head keeper told us that at night, under headlights, one dog had run down 116 rabbits within the hour. The down was scarred with white chalk entrenchments, and there were superb views of ripening grain over towards Andover. Bedlam is a primeval forest of oak, ash, and sycamore with recent introductions of spruce. Many trees were almost smothered by honeysuckle, with its beguiling drift of scent borne on the warm summer air.

Philip walked on through, and Bernard and I went round the outside, shouting and clapping our hands as we cut through at the top. We were rewarded with the sight of a Hobby. She glided out of the wood and over us, silent and imperturbed. Hobbies appear to have no nesting skills of their own; they appropriate the nests of other birds, most usually Crows. We failed to find a nest, though Philip scaled several of a number of possible trees. In any case the wood proved to be a poor photographic site. It was an enjoyable day.

July 22

Raymond and I, with the Kestrel perched on my handlebars, biked to Wishford after supper. We walked up to Ibsbury. The wood was wet and smelt deliciously of a mingling of honeysuckle, wood sage and calamint. As we came out on to the down by the earthworks, a roe deer ran up from below and jumped the wire netting into the wood. Coming back down from the hill, the moon, a third full hung low over Ibsbury. I saw it again from my bedroom window, suspended between two stars.

July 27

I joined the sheep dipping in Upper Woodford. Shep, Olly and assorted Kytes. About 60 sheep were cooped at a time, and driven along a narrow passage between hurdles, to the dip. The old 'Yowes', knowing what was coming, resisted stubbornly, but there was no escape from the evil-smelling, mustard-coloured liquid. It was oppressively hot, and the flies were crawling all over us!

July 30

The water meadows look at their splendid best. On both riverbanks runs a wide multi-coloured floral ribbon, consisting of the varied pinks of willow herb, bistort and purple loosestrife, and the very dissimilar yellow loosestrife, sharing names but not genus. Then there is mauve water peppermint, to which I am addicted. I like to carry a sprig to sniff. There are also great clumps of hemp agrimony and the purple and white bells of comfrey, much visited by bees. Finally, in one or two special places, bright yellow mimulus with its red freckled lip.

Canoeing down to Wild Duck Islands, (known to us as Widgeon and Teal, but more prosaically locally as Brown's Island), the river was almost at winter level. In order to avoid decapitation at the first bridge it was necessary to lie down quickly and let the currant carry me swiftly under both bridges. The bridges are only a few yards apart. The second bridge is wider and wooden, and is known as Cart Bridge. It leads to the old paper mill. When the Irish cattle are unloaded, they cross this bridge into the water meadows for rest and recuperation, before going on to Salisbury market. For several hours they are disorientated, and they bellow pitifully before settling down to feed on the lush herbage.

Soon after leaving the bridges, and just before the river bends way to the right and away from the lower road, there is shallow water and a gravel spit. Here, most summers it is necessary to disembark and assist the canoe to regain the deeper water. From there on the river flows swift and strong and deep, until the Islands are reached. Off Start Point, a Kingfisher sat on the end of a low hanging willow branch. It dived and came up with a silver minnow, then sped with it up the dividing channel. I have watched it fish from that point so many times. Kingfishers have the directness and speed of tiny missiles or arrowheads in flight. The bird's approaching ruddy breast quickly disappears into an iridescent streak of blue or green according to the angle of flight. Paddling back upstream was hard-going against the stiff current.

August 7

A fine day with a heat haze. Philip biked over early with the Merlin, and soon afterwards Bernard arrived and drove us over to Bulford Ranges to resume the search for the Hobby's nesting site. The Plain there is not good for flying hawks, not sufficiently open, too many higgledy-piggledy firs. Philip sent up the Merlin to draw out the Hobby, by acting as a lure. This was successful: almost immediately a Hobby shot out of a spruce. A lovely sight to watch as Hobby and Merlin rose higher and higher, baiting each other, finally vanishing into a far away beech clump.

We jumped back into the car and dashed off in pursuit. Philip climbed out and swung the lure (a rabbit's foot on a string), to no avail. That was the last we saw of the Merlin! However we did find the Hobby's nest on the outside of the spruce clump. Philip climbed up the nest tree, and Bernard puffed up the neighbouring tree. Both declared them perfect for a hide. The nest held three young Hobbies.

Later that day I canoed down to 'Wild Duck' again, this time with little Gerald. The river is still running deep, and the weeds need cutting. In the evening Philip and Bernard went to the ranges again to show Capt. Compton sport with the Merlin, but after the events of the morning, they had to take the Gos!

August 9

Philip has acquired a Sparrow Hawk of the dark variety. A most beautiful bird, quite perfect in every way, with its dark barred breast. He told me that the Merlin had flown down on the ranges, and some of the military had fed it on the fist, and then let it go again! Philip had asked them to tie it up.

August 10

I walked by Jean's barn, through the box wood to the dewpond, which was badly choked with rushes and parts of the old track were impenetrable from wild parsnip. Their flattish seeds resemble rolled oats, and crushed between the finger and thumb they give off a pleasant warm oily odour that reminds me of gorse. From Yarnbury

I watched five combines working within sight of each other. I hate to see trails of straw instead of hiles, but it does make harvesting so much quicker and easier.

I only saw two clouded yellow butterflies, and as for flowers, there was meadow cranesbill, with its delicate purple mauve blossoms, and common toadflax edging up the cultivated areas, its strong lemon flower with its striking orange lip set off by slim grey spikey leaves. Vervain is almost over-lookable, quite unremarkable in appearance, its tiny pale mauve flowers cluster on branched spiky stalks. It is an herb once valued for the protection it was supposed to give against witchcraft. There was autumn felwort, its tight erect buds just giving a hint of mauve, white horehound, the ubiquitous hieraciums, climbing melilot, and St John's wort, so called because it was supposed to open around St John's eve. Finally and quite the prettiest, musk mallow, rosy pink with ferny leaves, and slowly trodden under foot in the ruts, were the pale yellow flowers and silver grey feathery leaves of silverweed.

August 13

I walked in 'Para' for the last time. Taking Minerva with me, I let her loose and she flew off and made for a willow tree. I hope she will be all right. Near Robin Hood's bridge (a wooden plank fisherman's bridge), I watched a family of young Sedge Warblers. Mimulus was out and amphibious bistort. I took the Kestrel along with me, too, and she caught grasshoppers. Philip and Bernard were in the Kingfisher hide. Philip asked me over to view his latest acquisitions, a Hobby, which I did in the evening. It was about the size of a Kestrel, with fine dark moustachial streaks and ear coverts.

August 14

I let Jill off the leash for an hour. She flew round and round the house and garden, chasing the House Martins in play, and they twittered in mock alarm. As soon as I whistled and swung the lure she came at once to my fist for rabbit. She is very tame and several times I have taken her on a Wilts and Dorset bus, perched on my wrist, and she has shown no apprehension. I never hood her!

August 17

Alison and I took the Kestrel and hitched to Fovant. It was very squally with sunny intervals. We climbed up Chislebury, crossed the Old Coach Road, and went down by the five combs to Jeans' farm, Broadchalke. We sat on the down on hummocks of mingled thyme and rockrose, while Jill pecked at grasshoppers and lazy fat black beetles. She seemed a little frightened of the latter. We came back through

Stratford Tony, where we watched a little tabby kitten bounding over the stepping-stones. Climbing up Bishopstone Hill we saw several pairs of Bullfinches. They're always to be seen there, flitting along the overgrown blackthorn hedges. In winter, the vivid crimson breasts of the cocks, their black velvet caps, and white bands across the rump are unmissable..

Epilogue

My diary ends abruptly, two days before my wedding day on 19 August 1950, in St John's Church Bemerton, where my paternal grandmother and one of my aunts are buried. All our best wedding photographs were taken by Philip!

Two months later, the aunt's house was sold and to all intents and purposes all connection with Bemerton in South Wilts was ended. My husband and I spent five years at Nempnett Thrubwell and there my first son was born. From there we moved to Motcombe, near Shaftesbury, within sight of the Wiltshire downs, but the farm was on heavy clay in the Blackmore Vale. Another five years and two more children later – we were struck by foot-and-mouth disease. We had built up a good TT herd of high-yielding dairy shorthorn, which we had graded up to pedigree. Normally we made it our policy to avoid as far as possible buying in stock, preferring to breed our own. Now it was a cow bought in from a dispersal sale that started the outbreak. A most distressing time, possibly the worst moment being when the children's pet nanny goat was led out to be shot.

We re-stocked but sold out within the year and moved to Mere. I produced another daughter and switched from shorthorns to Guernseys, running up to twenty on ten acres, by strip grazing and buying in keep. In 1975 our fields were compulsory purchased by the local council for a housing estate.

All my life I had felt drawn to natural methods of farming, that nurtured the soil, returning to it what had been extracted from it. An excess of chemicals, I sensed, would in time poison the soil, the crops, and the animals, finally producing sick people. Many of the old farmworkers of the 'forties' had an instinctive distrust of what they disparagingly referred to as 'bag muck'. I was influenced by H.J. Massingham, who wrote passionately about the old country ways and methods of farming. He wrote of an old order for which the sands were fast running out. Then came Frank Newman-Turner who opened a new chapter with his fertility farming and pleas for organic methods. He took a lot of stick and ridicule because he was out of kilter with the times. He was in a very real sense a corner stone of the Organic Movement.

We tried in a modest way to farm without chemicals, and used herbal remedies such as garlic for mastitis. We sowed herbal leys produced by Newman-Turner in partnership with Juliet de Baracli Levi, a herbalist. *As well as a variety of meadow grasses, they contained deep-rotting herbs that brought up minerals from the subsoil, such as chicory and the humble dandelion. The fashionable ley mixtures of the time had very few grasses. There were cock's foot and Timothy, perennial rye grass and red clover. Turned into a ley, it was noticeable how often cows made for these hedgerow 'weeds'.*

My life has been exceedingly obscure, and undoubtedly the best days were those spent in an unspoilt countryside with decent, uncomplicated country people.

Glossary

Bents – Stiff dried grass and flower stalks.

A Bury – This was the term used for a warren or rabbit burrow.

Caddling – A good old Wiltshire word for something unpleasant such as bad weather or being on cavan!

Cavan or **Cavings** – The husks and dusty rubbish ejected by the threshing machine which separated the grain from the chaff. 'To be on Cavan' was to be clearing it up, an unpleasant job. The air was full of dust and no masks were worn. I suspect the word to have been of saxon origin.

Cob – Is the name for a male swan, the female being a pen.

Fourgrain – A four pronged fork used for forking up dung and for spreading it on to the fields.

Hiling – Pronounced 'ai-ling ', was the Wiltshire term for what in other counties was called, stooking or stitching. When corn was cut, the loose corn went through a machine called a binder, which was originally attached to horses and later tractors. This bound the loose corn into sheaves, which were then ejected on to the field. These were picked up by the labourers two at a time. They clashed the heads together while at the same time, fixing the butts firmly on the ground. Usually six sheaves formed an hile. The corn like this was left out to dry, sometimes for weeks. After wet weather the sheaves would have to be thrown apart to dry out and then put back together again when dry. Finally they would be pitched on to wagons pulled by horses or tractors and taken to the rick yard or designated site for building the rick.

'Para' – Short for 'Paradise' my designation for the water-meadows lying approximately to the west of Broken Bridges, bounded by Wilton Park Wall and 14 Hatches.

Pooks – When dry the wakes were rolled up with a prong into pooks, making a small stack, easy for pitching on to the wagon.

Prong – A two-grained pitchfork used in hay making and for pitchforking hay or sheaves of corn on to wagons or ricks.

Tegs – These are young rams.

A trip – Of pigs, sometimes called a farrowing or litter.

Vallum – The steep walls or banks of earthworks such as Old Sarum.

Wakes – Lines of grass, which had been mown for hay and left in the sun to dry